# CAMPING
## FOR YOUNG PEOPLE

by Anthony Greenbank

HARRAP LONDON

First published in Great Britain 1979
by GEORGE G. HARRAP & CO LTD
182–184 High Holborn, London WC1V 7AX

© Anthony Greenbank 1979

ISBN 0 245 53260 9

*Filmset by Woolaston Parker Ltd, Leicester*
*Printed in Great Britain by offset lithography by*
*Billing & Sons Limited, Guildford, London and Worcester*

For Grant,
8th. March 1981.
with love from
Dad.

# CAMPING
## FOR YOUNG PEOPLE

# Contents

## IMPERIAL AND METRIC EQUIVALENTS

*Weight*

| | |
|---|---|
| 1 ounce | 28·350 grams |
| 1 pound | 0·4536 kilogram |
| 1 ton | 1016 kilograms |
| 1 kilogram | 2·2046 pounds |

*Linear measure*

| | |
|---|---|
| 1 inch | 2·54 centimetres |
| 1 foot | 0·3048 metre |
| 1 yard | 0·9144 metre |
| 1 mile | 1·6093 kilometres |
| 1 centimetre | 0·3937 inch |
| 1 metre | 3·2808 feet |
| 1 kilometre | 0·6214 mile |

# 1　How to Use this Book

This book is about LIGHTWEIGHT CAMPING—sleeping out in the safest possible way for ordinary young people. It does not intend to turn you into a sourdough, however—the American word for a backwoodsman who might dry out wet boots by the very effective method of filling them with porridge oats so the leather does not shrink or become hard, and then eating them (the oats, not the boots). Nor at the other extreme does it encourage the kind of camping where you take along the teapot. What it does show instead is how to spend nights out for next to nothing in marvellous surroundings. And how to use the minimum of equipment, yet be comfortable while doing so in any but the wildest weather and quite possibly in remote areas too. Later is the time to specialise if, in fact, you wish to camp differently.

Camping should be a means to an end when you are young. The popularity of outdoor pastimes like canoeing, cycling, angling, climbing, backpacking, bird watching, scuba diving, potholing, surfing, hang gliding and so on, involve young people most of all. No other form of accommodation gives the same flexibility, mobility, independence, freedom or low cost to go with these activities as camping. You are spending mental, nervous and physical energy through the day, and camp is simply a roof over your head, somewhere to cook supper and breakfast and a place to recharge your batteries. That many such camp sites are in wild and beautiful regions is an added bonus.

There will be times, however, when you may have to camp among hundreds of other tents. In parts of the world noted for the spectacular scenery there, local by-laws direct all campers to certain sites, so congested is the immediate region with holiday-makers. Not that this need put you off. There are always thousands of other spots where—with appropriate permission—you can camp alone: by mountain pools, along sea-shore surf, in desolate glens, among the deepest forest, on friendly knolls, near flowering meadows . . .

Whatever your reasons for camping, the nub of the matter is the same: how, by knowing what you are about, you can spend your nights as safely as if inside bricks and mortar, and still live as you would on one of those commercial camp sites with its hot and cold water, showers, lavatories and the rest. This book helps to that end by detailing camping experiments which, if you practise them carefully, should give you a head start in tackling camping with competence and purpose, yet which will guide you clear of the rash mistakes made far from home by beginners who become a victim of their energy and ambition.

These experiments will help you find your feet in the comfort of home and neighbourhood. You do, however, require patience and application to carry them through. And a little ingenuity, too. And you must always look on the more serious ones as the real thing. Forget that you may fail time and again in a number of these camping situations even when you are only practising them. Instead, give them everything you can just as if your safety and enjoyment during a 'pitch' were involved (as one day, if the camping bug bites, it really will).

Begin here. The first experiment is a simple demonstration of the need to employ 'systems' when camping, yet it is none the less apt for that. Economy is a product of these systems—whether mental, muscular or nervous effort. Or financial cost. In this instance, it's that cost—and peace of mind.

*How do you come to terms with a jukebox that swamps conversation and pierces the eardrums when it is playing a kind of music you might detest—say country and western or reggae? And you must stay within its range? It's not easy. The volume of a modern jukebox is extremely powerful. The bass notes thumping from the speaker are near perfect—much better than domestic radio, TV or stereo units. So look for the record nearest to your tastes on the selection card. There will usually be one, and now you can begin the system. It will most likely cost 5p to play this record once and have three minutes of relatively blissful peace. But three minutes might be nowhere nearly enough. You will want to play the same track again. But be careful. Jukeboxes have pitfalls which can trap the inexperienced. You must not stab impatiently at the buttons because you could waste your coins. Many jukeboxes offer a choice of three records for 10p. But this doesn't mean you can play your favourite three times in a row. Say the number of the record is Q8 on the selection card and you press Q8 three times before the disc has started to spin. Your chosen record will only play once. The reason is that the jukebox has only a short memory. It remembers only the first push of any one record. The most you can hope for from your 10p is two consecutive plays of your choice—six minutes of freedom from the other noise! And you do it like this. Drop your 10p in the slot and press Q8. Wait until the disc is spinning. Then press Q8 again. You cannot press Q8 yet again because the machine won't register it. So select one more record you can at least tolerate. There should be at least another on the selection card. AND if you want to play the current number one record, be careful that someone else hasn't already pushed its buttons. If they have, your selection won't register for the same reason just described. You must wait for the top disc to spin before you press it again.*

OK? The fact is that, like this, your system will make life that much more comfortable and enjoyable away from home. And all home's conveniences are taken so much for granted until you actually hit the camping trail. Yet this experiment, like others in this book, is not as far removed from travelling with a tent as you might think. Outdoor enthusiasts are inevitably trapped at one time or other in pub or cafe waiting for the storm to stop, for companions to join them or just while recovering from the day's walking, canoeing or whatever. And if the jukebox has a crumby selection, well . . . It is the same with other experiments listed, from learning how much easier it is to pitch your tent correctly by chewing peanuts the while, to making the most of your room inside the tent in the same way that occupants of nuclear submarines and space voyagers have to do. Systems one and all.

But there is a snag. It is too easy to become over-confident as you discover these experiments—some of which include sleeping out for next to no cost—do indeed work, and your proficiency at performing them grows. Done as they are, first of all, in safe surroundings, it is easy to gain the impression that that is all there is to it. And a tyro at this stage cannot wait to head for the big country of moors, lakes and mountains, only to find . . . that camping in bad weather is very different from when the sun shines. And that this really sorts the men out from the boys. Indeed not only can it put you off camping for good, but it could also prove dangerous. The change-over from backyard experiments to the testing grounds of outback camp sites far removed from home needs care and responsibility.

This book, I hope, will instil such a sense of reason with which to probe the unknown safely and yet lose none of the sense of adventure. You can indeed find the joy of keeping warm and snug while in your capsule of warm air, separated by material only a fraction of an inch thick from the downpour outside, and wake next morning to find the air all the fresher as you prepare to continue on your way. Every effort has been made to keep instructions clear and simple, but it is strongly suggested that a young reader should ask advice and approval from a responsible adult before trying any but the simplest experiments. Take care, even at this stage.

# 2 Trial Offer Camping

All you need for camping is a tent, sleeping bag and cooking equipment. Not much when you say it quickly, but these items must be of the best quality to give most enjoyment and safety. Quality in the camping field does not come cheaply.

A huge choice of these items awaits you at outdoor supply shops. You might still buy the best—only to discover later that it is unsuitable for your purposes and you have wasted your money. It is important therefore to look on camping kit from the point of view of the people actually designing it in the first place. To this end you can't do better than camp out near home using home-made tackle. This kind of inexpensive start will then offer invaluable insight into what and what not to buy—and the right questions to ask when the time comes to buy camping accessories.

## THE FIRST NIGHT'S TRIAL

The methods which follow may not cost much, but they are—followed correctly—safe. And if in fact you don't fancy camping after all, having tried them (and in spite of them), then you won't have wasted money buying costly tents and things first. But give them every chance: like waiting for fine weather, going only with friends and taking pains to find a pleasant camp site. Otherwise you might not enjoy the experience at all.

First, you need a field laboratory: a piece of flat grass like a lawn or field. Villages and towns give plenty of scope here, but if you live in a city you may have to look rather further afield. Parks and commons are too public and not advised; in any case camping would normally not be allowed. But a visit to your local library will help. Ask to see guidebooks and maps of the surrounding countryside, and they should soon reveal rough country somewhere on the city limits a bus ride away and where, after you have asked permission from the nearest farm, nobody will bother you.

It's always best to go with others keen to try camping. If you are too young to make such ventures on your own, an older person will have to go with you. But even older young people should take a companion or two along with them as a psychological help. Spending your first night below the stars can be a spooky experience without the reassurance of others nearby.

Fine weather is a must. Although the tent you are about to make for a song will stop the rain, a warm dry night will prove more comfortable and safer. So check the radio weather forecast first.

Collect the items needed—as detailed below—and pack them in a cycle bag, rucksack, duffle bag or anything else appropriate. Do this even when you are going to camp on the lawn as it is easier to have everything at hand from the start—just as you would on a real camping trip. In such cases make a bet with yourself that you will keep out of your house until the next morning—having succeeded in cooking your supper and breakfast on your first night out. Make this rule from the time you actually pitch your tent. Like now. . . .

### Make a Hang Glider tent

This little shelter vibrates and hums in the breeze like a hang glider, as do most modern lightweight tents. The days of flapping canvas are long gone, or should be if today's tents are pitched correctly. Then they give all the appearance of straining to take off into the sky like a kite. Instead, you pull them down, anchor them to the ground and sleep under their cover.

The Hang Glider Experimental tent is in fact a tube tent, which can be used in an emergency just about anywhere—providing there is shelter in the lee of a wall, boulder or sharp dip in the ground so shielding it from the wind. This kind of shelter has proved popular in America where the seemingly endless sunshine makes carrying a tent which packs into little more space than a couple of maps good sense; just polythene tubing, in fact. While, in my earlier book, *Survival for Young*

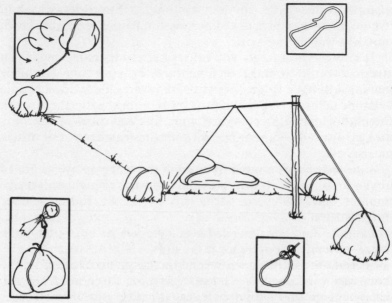

*The Hang Glider Experimental Tent*

*People*, I detailed several kinds of shelter made from plastic sheeting, the tube tent is different for our purpose because it uses stronger material and incorporates a groundsheet built into the rest of the refuge—like any good tent today, in fact.

A WORD ABOUT PLASTIC SHEETING, HOWEVER. NOT BECAUSE YOU NEED DOUBT ITS STRENGTH, BUT BECAUSE, ONCE IT DOES TEAR, THE TENDENCY IS TO LEAVE IT LYING RATHER THAN PACK IT AWAY. DO TAKE IT WITH YOU WHEN YOU GO. AND REMEMBER THAT IF YOU MAKE A HABIT OF CAMPING UNDER PLASTIC IT DOES LACK PRIVACY. AT LEAST TENT MATERIAL WILL SCREEN ROVING EYES FROM SEEING YOUR CAMERA AND OTHER VALUABLES IF YOU TAKE AN EVENING WALK FROM YOUR CAMP.

First you need the plastic tubing. Go to a garden centre or warehouse selling plastic sheeting (look in the yellow pages of your phone book to check where there is one near you), and ask for six or seven feet of 500-gauge heavy duty polythene tubing: 48in across. You may be lucky enough to arrive as they start a new roll where the first few feet may have one or two punctures. That's still fine for your purposes. Ask for this and they might

give you it for a few pence (they usually throw it away). But
even the unflawed plastic tubing is not expensive, and it will
cost less than £1.

Then collect the rest of the items. You need a really strong
stick about 4ft long; plenty of thick strong 'hairy' string; a
penknife to cut it with; two or three pebbles; four big rocks so
hefty—as shown—that you can hardly get your arms around
them; three meat skewers; and three 'visclamps' which you can
make from pieces of coat hanger wire and which are bent with a
pair of pliers into a shape like a keyhole (see diagram).

Choose the site for your hang glider tent on ground where no
obvious stones are lying embedded in the grass, and where
pools of water are unlikely to collect if it rains. It should also be
in the shelter of something large which protects it from the
wind—like a house, shed, barn or gorse bushes but—as we see
later—never under trees.

Spread the polythene tube on the grass, take the end away
from any wind as your entrance, and at three points, equal
distances apart, secure pebbles into the edge of the plastic with
the visclamps as shown (visclamps are actually a USA
invention which use small rubber balls, but small stones are
just as good). Pass a meat skewer each through two of the
visclamps and pin them to the ground—again, as shown. At
this stage avoid dragging the plastic too taut between them.
Time enough to align everything tightly later.

To cut the coat hanger wire is easy: place the wire between
the wire-cutting blade in the jaws of the pliers and tap on top of
the tool with a hammer. Then, still holding the pliers fast, bend
the wire sharply up and down with your other hand and it will
suddenly snap off.

Draw the opposite end of the tube together in a fist and knot
string around it, pulling it fast. Tie the string to a visclamp and
skewer this to the ground so that, in effect, the triangular floor
of the tent is now marked out on the ground.

Tie a long piece of strong string next to the remaining
visclamp at the entrance; twist this three times round the top of
the stick which is then pushed into the ground like a vertical
tent pole, but several inches away from the tent itself. Now
walk backwards keeping the string tight and the shelter raised,
and wind this several times around that heavy rock before

finally tying off the end. After heaving this anchor further away from the entrance the shelter should now stand wobbling, but pitched.

Incidentally, the diagram shows the alternative way of making the ridge in the tent. Here a long piece of string passes beneath the plastic from the tail of the shelter up to where it is wrapped around the stick. It is anchored to the ground by meat skewers and, as we see below, a large rock as well. And the end of the tent is tied together by a separate bit of string. Either way, however, will work; it just depends which you find easiest to do.

Relocate the skewers so the groundsheet is flat and not puckered. Then reinforce the anchorage of each corner of the tent by tying four feet of string to each visclamp on the ground. The other end of each piece of string is then wound round (and knotted) one of the big rocks which should now be trundled into place (*they should be too heavy to lift*) so, keeping the string taut, you roll each rock with the string wound round it on to the meat skewer and visclamp. The combined pull of rock and visclamp now make the plastic really secure.

Now adjust the tent pole—it helps if someone holds it—and drag the anchoring rock into the final position which keeps everything upright, balanced and taut. And certainly fit to sleep inside for a night. This last rock, by the way, should be the biggest of the four.

### Make an insulating pad

Cover the top of the groundsheet with dead ferns, leaves, hay, heather, grasses etc. Next, spread newspapers over these until all you can see is overlapping print.

Incidentally, there is one improvement to be made if you have an old cycle inner tube. Blow a little air into this and place it—folded like a squib, and held in this shape by rubber bands—where your hips will be. It will greatly add to your comfort when you slide inside your home-made sleeping bag which is actually your next stage of things to do but one.

But first collect your cooking gear. Arrange the few bits and pieces you need to cook a meal to one side of the doorway so that, when you are lying inside the tent, you can cook from the comfort of your sleeping bag. It's the lightweight camping way of doing things; a system used by explorers, climbers and sundry other adventurers for many years now.

### The multi-candle-power safety burner

Find a tin can big enough to cook your supper, and this will be your cooking pot. In fact you should try it out at home first on the kitchen stove to check just how much food it will hold. It should be large enough, say, to boil a couple of eggs at the same time, or to hold enough stewing steak or something like that with room to spare. Nothing fancy; just the essentials. You then need another tin which is rather bigger so the cooking pot will slide inside it freely but with not too much room to spare. This can now be made into your cooker.

For the pot simply take a Stanley knife and with the point of the sharp blade pierce two small holes near the top and opposite each other. Push a piece of coat hanger wire through these so the result is a curved 'bail' or handle as shown. To enlarge the holes made by the Stanley knife, simply twist the knife blade (or push the narrow point of a pair of scissors through the original small holes and enlarge by twisting).

The illustration shows how you cut the tin can for the stove. Again a Stanley knife will cut away the larger flaps of metal. And will *start* all the holes. But only start them. To enlarge the holes to the large-ish size illustrated do it by twisting that sharp narrow point of a pair of scissors through the metal—pushing all the while.

First, though, cut four triangular flaps in the bottom of the tin so you can then bend them upwards inside the can like spikes. Then push a candle down on to each of these. It depends on the size of the tin really as to how many candles you do use. With larger cans, for instance, you might even make it five candles for that much quicker heating.

Next completely cut away the big flaps around the base of the can walls so that a good draught can pass through and boost the candle flames. You can now make the holes through the rest of the metal. These serve two purposes: to afford more air holes AND also so you can push two pieces of coat hanger wire through them on which to rest the cooking pot.

This height must be adjustable. As the candles burn lower you will then be able to take out the wires and push them

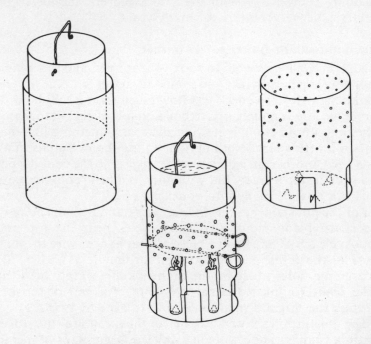

*The Multi Candle Power Safety Burner*

through holes lower down the can sides so the pot is always at just the right height above the candle flames. This is important for the most efficient burning. Also remember that when you take the wires out to re-position them, they will be hot. So curve one end of each wire with a pair of pliers as shown, and you can then hold these handles between a piece of cloth.

NEEDLESS TO SAY YOU SHOULD USE A LARGE STONE (OR STONES) AS A WINDSHIELD WHEN USING THIS STOVE. AND NEVER USE IT INSIDE YOUR TENT. YOU CAN MOREOVER MAKE QUITE SURE IT IS NOT ACCIDENTALLY KNOCKED OVER DURING YOUR COOKING SIMPLY PIN IT TO GRASS BY HAMMERING MEAT SKEWERS AROUND THE BASE INTO THE GROUND SO IT IS LOCKED FIRMLY UPRIGHT IN POSITION.

**Pots & pans**

The fewer the better should be your attitude to cooking utensils. All you need are: a plastic mug; a set of KFS (knife/fork/spoon); a lid for the cooking pot to make things inside heat faster; a foldable wire handle attached to this lid; a plastic bowl to serve as dish and plate; plastic orange squash bottle filled with fresh water; and that's it.

You need enough candles to fuel your burner; half a dozen, say, cut in half. As for matches, carry them inside a film cassette container together with a strip of sandpaper for a striking surface. So that the match heads don't accidentally rub together and ignite, place half the matches head down, the rest head up. An extra precaution: dip each match head in hot candle wax first which forms a waterproof varnish.

**Wrap a Klondyke bedroll**

A few old blankets will keep you warm during a fine night's camping in your Hang Glider tent. The design described only works well, however, when more layers of blanket end up beneath you than on top. It also helps if you can lay your hands on a cellular blanket. Most blankets will be of the close-woven type, but a cellular blanket spread between them will make you all the warmer as it traps warm air in the cells sandwiched between the other blankets.

Make the bedroll just outside the entrance of the tent. The first blanket is laid on the ground, and will eventually be the outer layer. Now place half of the next blanket across the first—the cellular blanket, in fact, if you have one. Half the third blanket is then spread across the second blanket, but the rest of it overlaps in the other direction—as can be seen from the diagram.

Fold the third blanket over the first, then the second and finally the first. Pin the blankets together down the side with blanket pins or baby pins with a safety clasp. Finally fold the bottom of the bedroll up and pin this, too.

Before climbing into it take stock of the temperature. If you have another blanket and then decide the evening is not quite as warm as you expected, fold that blanket double and place it beneath the bedroll. Any extra bedding needs to go under rather than on top.

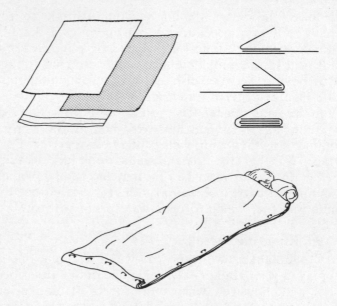

*The Klondyke Blanket Bedroll*

## Test a cooking system (supper)

Cook supper before you go to sleep. Choose only the food you like, and cook it more or less to the order shown below. It is learning how to use the minimum of utensils which is important.

The first thing is to don your sleeping gear—some clothing and woollen socks (a pair of long football socks, say). Wriggle down between the blankets, then caterpillar the bedroll (with you inside it) into the tent by alternately lifting your back off the ground then shuffling the blankets forward with your legs until you are comfortably right inside the shelter.

Wrap your trousers and anything else soft inside a sweater and use this as a pillow. This actually becomes an elbow rest as you then prepare your food on the cooker which will burn outside on the grass.

Light the cooker and place the billy can on top. Only fill it a third full, however. This will boil more quickly. You can make a cup of instant coffee or tea, replace the water left back on top of the burner and then top it up with more cold water which will then heat even faster—thanks to the water already bubbling in the container. Now add the two eggs you might have chosen for supper, or the tin of baked beans and sausages or even—but only if you have made a large cooker and pot for this one—the plastic sachet of roast beef and gravy or cod with cheese sauce (and in which case you can, as this plastic bag is sealed, add a spud or two and some salt to the boiling water, not to mention the odd carrot as well) to the boiling water. When the fifteen minutes cooking time is up you will already have had a warm drink, so you can now eat your meal and still have more water boiling by the time you finish for another drink. And have enough hot water warming up again for the washing up, not that hot water is even necessary unless fatty food has been cooked, as we see later: cold water will do. The water will boil quicker, incidentally, if you keep the lid on top (with a little space left so that steam can escape).

**Sleeping systems**

Partly block the tent entrance with rucksack, branches, stones—anything handy to check the wind if it changes direction overnight. Place matches, candle and torch by your side where you can find them at once. Tuck your head below the blankets and breathe into them. If you still feel drowsy read yourself to sleep. Imagine your tent panels are in fact parachute panels and that you are floating away.

Certain things, however, might still keep you awake. Noises in the night, for instance. A tree branch creaking, grass rustling or a distant owl hooting might sound ominous at first. Your imagination runs riot. Expect such distractions and try to look on them as normal. Gradually you should doze off. And, anyway, wasn't that why your friends are sleeping next door in their tents (for mutual support)?

Wind is another distraction. Here you can do something concrete like going outside and placing heavy rocks over the skewers—just in case. Reinforcing the 'door' at the tent entrance can also increase your peace of mind simply because you shut most of the draught out.

Two more tips: if you feel cold, wear your hat as much of your body heat escapes through your bare head; and when you roll over, turn with the bedroll rather than try to move inside it.

### Cooking (breakfast)

Use the same system as before. Reach out from the blankets, pull the burner to just the other side of the threshold and light it. Boil some water in the bottom of the billy, and pour yourself a cup of coffee or whatever. Now add more water—enough to make the porridge which has been standing overnight soaking in your plastic bowl and which you now tip into the container. Eat this as the water heats again, this time to boil your couple of eggs. And the egg water can then be used as a second hot drink.

### Striking camp

Pack away your gear in the reverse order you took it out and set it up (and wrap up the Hang Glider tent after shaking it free of dew or raindrops). Untie the string from the big stone and stamp down any disturbed earth where you skewered the shelter to the ground. Pick up every scrap of matchstick, silverfoil, eggshell and other rubbish; and pour greasy water only on to soil—not grass. Take litter home with you, including tin cans which can be smashed flat between stones to save space.

## THE SECOND NIGHT'S TEST

Follow up the first night out with a second one. Only use rather different items, and another approach; one where you take tent and sleeping bag only, and no food to cook. Instead eat a good meal before you go, packing only instant edibles like a Mars Bar, some raisins and peanuts with, say, a vacuum flask of your favourite hot drink to top the list. Then all you need do is reach your camp site, pitch your tent and bed down with your paperback.

The same safety rules still apply: check weather forecast first; go with others rather than alone; and obtain permission to set up camp. What is different in this case, however, is the kind of tent you make first. And the sleeping bag which also needs careful preparation.

## Make a Timberline Experimental tent

The Timberline tent is named after an actual class of tent—like the Meadow tent, the High Mountain tent, the Arctic tent and the Wet Mountain. As its name suggests it can be used on the more exposed camp sites, though it would still be vulnerable on the toughest situations where only the high mountain tent—which does not apply to this book anyway—would be able to survive. The 'timberline' tent in fact falls somewhere between the 'meadow' tent and the 'high mountain' model, and its design has several important features as a result.

It has, for instance, a flysheet which is a second tent constructed over the first. This flysheet (or fly, as it is known) has a porch which shelters the inner tent entrance. It will have a sewn-in, or fitted, groundsheet, so excluding draughts and insects. And A-poles will often be used—the tent supports which, instead of being tent poles placed vertically, prop up the shelter by straddling it just like an 'A' to give the structure more stability and extra room for those inside to move about.

Our Timberline Experimental tent—as illustrated—follows this pattern with two exceptions. One is the flysheet does not actually come down to touch the ground, because it simply isn't big enough—you are after all using up your plastic tube used for the Hang Glider tent. And the groundsheet in this case is a separate sheet of plastic rather than an integral part of the tent (as it would be if you were to buy this type of shelter). This is because you can then re-use the plastic sheet already used for the Hang Glider tent, but which is not quite big enough to offer you a fitted groundsheet as well with the timberline design. This, however, is no bad thing at this stage of affairs; you will still learn valuable lessons by using the separate ground covering.

Firstly, tie the end of some really strong string to a wall, railing or even a tree (normally taboo for camping under, but as you have a fine weather forecast the foliage will not probably drip on you in the night). The string should be about two feet from the grass at this point, and you now walk backwards pulling the string tight, then wind it at a higher level around the junction of the two sticks—each about five-feet long and lashed together first to make a primitive kind of A-pole—which straddle the tent door so that you can pass between them to the inside of the shelter. Keep backing away as you pull on the string, then anchor this down to the ground around a very heavy rock as you did for the Hang Glider tent.

The A-pole, meanwhile, will probably have fallen down. The best way to support this is for someone to hold it upright for the moment. The A-pole, however, can be kept upright if you are on your own by sticking the ends into the ground, adjusting the sticks vertically once more under the pull of the string, then adjusting the rock's position again.

Now take the flysheet and inner tent material. The flysheet, as we have said, is simply your old Hang Glider tent of strong polythene; you just slit it down the middle so forming one large sheet of plastic instead of a tube. The inner tent, however, needs to be a material which breathes like an old cotton sheet, curtain or flag, say, cut to a size of 6ft × 8ft.

The order in which you arrange this two-skinned tent is left to you for now (reason later). Whichever way you go about it—it's easy. Simply follow the diagram which shows how the flysheet is folded over the string and secured to the ground with visclamps, string and heavy stones at the corners and also, in this case, along the bottom edges, so the material cannot flap. By adjusting the stones as the tent progresses the plastic is pulled tighter than you could do with meat skewers for anchors.

And the inner tent? This is not folded over the string but, instead, is hooked up to it by the following simple method: fold the cotton sheet in half so the two six-foot edges form the tent sides and the eight-foot sides are folded in half to make the inner tent roof. Now do the hooking-up which means simply placing a visclamp at each end of the centre fold, then tying a thin nylon shoe lace to each visclamp and finally knotting the two shoe laces to the string with prusik knots. As these are knots which can be slid into place when not under pressure, but which lock solid once they are pulled tight, you simply slide them outwards along the string away from the inner tent. And the inner tent hangs down ready to be pegged out. If this inside tent sags in the middle, incidentally, it can be hooked up to the

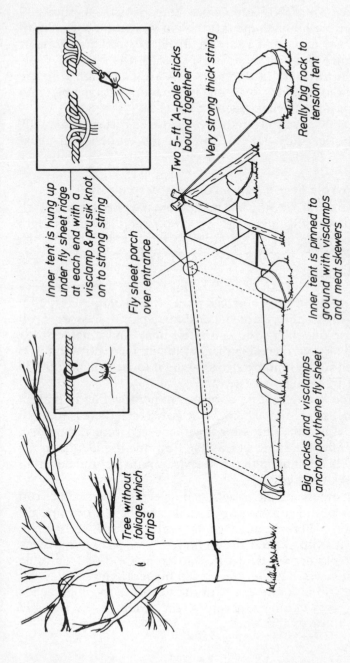

Inner tent is hung up under fly sheet ridge at each end with a visclamp & prusik knot on to strong string

Two 5-ft 'A-pole' sticks bound together

Very strong thick string

Really big rock to tension tent

Fly sheet porch over entrance

Inner tent is pinned to ground with visclamps and meat skewers

Big rocks and visclamps anchor polythene fly sheet

Tree without foliage, which drips

Fly sheet is not supposed to touch inner tent

*The Timberline Experimental Tent*

string above simply by adding visclamps which—as shown—
are bent into a hook-shape rather than the keyhole used until
now. A final note: make sure the flysheet overlaps the inner
tent entrance as much as possible to form the porch.

The bottom edges of the inner tent are next pinned to the
ground with visclamps (attached to the cloth with pebbles and
to the ground with meat skewers).

As for the separate groundsheet . . . Use a rectangle of really
strong plastic, and staple it down at the corners with meat
skewers.

## The disposable brown paper Hayloft Sleeping Bag

An experimental sleeping bag made from paper is not new. U.S.
marines have used them, and when you think of the strength
of a large paper sack of potatoes—well, it must be possible.
And there is no fire risk here either as there is no cooking
during this project.

The sleeping bag can be made in an evening. All you need are
plenty of sheets of tough brown paper (from old parcels, say),
50-pence-worth of hay from a pet shop, a pair of scissors, a roll
of sellotape one-inch wide and a felt pen. And a helper too.

Lay the hay out on newspaper in the sun. Or a warm room. It
cannot be too dry, and by also shaking it loose in handfuls you
get rid of irritating dust.

Sellotape enough sheets of brown paper together to make a
single panel so big that when you lie down on it there is room to
spare. Having done this, stick together—separately, though—
another panel the same size as the first one. Incidentally, the
paper sheets making up the two separate panels should overlap
each other at the edges.

Lie flat on one of the panels as if asleep so your helper can
trace your outline on the paper—keeping the felt pen upright
during this. There is no need to trace around your head,
however; just up around the shoulders and across your neck
will do. Now draw round this outline again, but from nine
inches out so the new outline is even bigger than you. It is this
silhouette you now clip out with the scissors and which, when
finished, gives a long tapering shape, wide at the top and
narrower towards the foot.

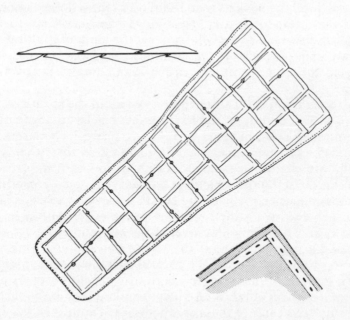

*The Hayloft Sleeping Bag*

Take this cutout and press it on top of the other brown paper panel—either with your friend holding it down or by weighting it with books or bricks. Trace round its outline, then cut out the second similar size panel.

Make the rest of the sleeping bag in a warm room, and with a solid wood surface on which you can press hard when sellotaping. As the diagram shows, each panel of brown paper is now covered—front and back—with pockets of more brown paper, each 12-inches square and each compartment holding a couple of handfuls of warm dry hay (do NOT fill the pockets too full, incidentally, or the bag will never fold and will come apart more easily). Not only should the pockets on one side overlap the pockets on the other side of each panel, but you should also leave enough space between the pockets on any one side so that the sellotape holding down the edges of one pocket does not touch the sellotape holding another on the same side. Otherwise all the pockets tend to lift off as the sellotape unpeels with the strain of it all. Work slowly and carefully to the pattern shown, and you will soon get the hang of quilting the brown paper panels so the cushioned surfaces on one side overlap those of the other—rather than completely covering them.

Although you can pad to the very edges of the mouth of the sleeping bag, do not let the hay pockets reach the sides or the bottom of the two big panels. You need a two-inch margin on both sides of each panel clear of padding so that when you finally attach the two panels together, you can press really hard on the sellotape which sticks them together—something not possible when the padding gets in the way. It helps, in fact, to attach the two panels first along the edges with a paper stapler, and then sellotape over these wire clips.

Make a final check that the sellotaping is sound—always running both thumbs (or the back of a Stanley knife or some other smooth rounded object) hard over the adhesive strip to guarantee a firm bond. It also helps to take a needle and thread and stitch 'buttons' of thick cardboard each about the size of a penny and with two holes through the middle AND sew these in pairs on opposite sides of the paper at salient points along the edges of the pockets where the sellotape could so easily peel away. As the buttons are sewn back to back in pairs quite separately from each other they really add to the overall strength of the bag. And because they are made of cardboard they don't tear as easily as if you were to stitch the thread through the brown paper alone.

The bag has now to be rolled ready for carrying to your second camp site in a large polythene bag inside your rucksack, cycle bag or whatever. But only do this just before setting out. And take a roll of sellotape, some cardboard buttons, needle and thread and some spare pieces of brown paper with you for running repairs.

# 3 Mistakes you might have made

Camping is the same as any new skill—you learn best by making mistakes. The fact that your tent blew down, the plastic rattled like a mainsail or the door let in the damp would do you no harm at all, especially as your equipment has so far cost next to nothing. And, like fighter pilot trainees who bungle their simulator controls and crash, it is nowhere near as expensive as buying equipment straight away only to find it is not the right kind.

Experiencing the wrong way of going about things first, then having to put it right yourself is, in fact, a much more effective way of learning than having an instructor stand over your every move and telling you how with a 'Right, lads, watch me pitch this tent, then you can do it' approach. This way just doesn't register later when you are about to go wrong on your own, and there is nobody to say 'no'.

Where did you go wrong? Several times, I hope, if you tried the last chapter's experiments correctly—that is, without running for help whenever you failed. Admit the times when your face was red, however, and you will be better prepared to know what you want in the way of camping equipment than ever before. Then you won't end up taking someone else's word for it—mine, for instance.

## HANG GLIDER TENT FLOPS

Both the shape and materials of this small tent simulate the kind of tent used by backpackers requiring the very lightest form of shelter, and which can be packed into the smallest space. The tapered floor and sloping roof ensured minimum bulk; the plastic skin, a waterproof cone weighing rather less than a bag of sugar. Yet only one-skin thick.

How your polythene tent actually fared should have given you an idea of the camping involved—a compact kind of living where the smallest detail must not be overlooked.

### The tent did fall down. Frequently . . .

The rock anchoring the guy line at the front of the shelter was not heavy enough to take the strain. It would skid over the grass under the pull from the string, and so the tent would slip out of alignment and collapse.

Tents made from one thickness of nylon also look flimsy enough to fall over easily, yet when pitched properly—as your plastic tent would have stood had you used a heavier rock—can be most weatherproof, even in strong winds. But you have to work at pitching them.

### And flap? You could hardly sleep for the noise

Nylon tents—like your polythene tent—are more noisy and 'lively' than tents of proofed cotton, the old standby of campers which has been replaced by lighterweight materials. The sloping roof design also rattles in the wind more than does a tent with a horizontal ridge. The trouble is that nylon soon sags. So you can expect to have to adjust it as wrinkle-free as glass whenever you camp, taking pains with guys and pegs to achieve this.

Tent manufacturers have tried different solutions to quieten down noisy tents. The most popular method is to use a ridgepole which runs from tent pole to tent pole immediately below the ridge of the tent, and so gives a much greater structural strength to the shelter. Another is to design tent panels with a 'catenary cut' so the shape of the ridge is actually curved like a well-loaded clothes line. It too helps stop tent flutter and sagging.

### You tore the groundsheet within moments

And probably could not help it. Groundsheets made from the same relatively lightweight material as the tent are vulnerable. It is worth always checking that the groundsheet of any tent you intend buying is made of a heavier material. Some tents have, but not all. It's important.

### Your Klondyke bedroll was wet next morning
Even though it did not rain . . .

The reason was you blocked up the tent entrance too well, in case it rained or the wind changed in the night. Yet if you had done this with many single skin nylon tents on the market, the same thing would have happened. With many? You could say with them all! Indeed leaving the door wide open would have kept you drier (so long as it did not rain).

As a tent can make a difference of some 10 degrees C. between the inside and outside temperatures, warm air on the inside of a tent will condense on the chilled inner tent walls during the cool of the night. Small droplets cling to the nylon or, as in your case, polythene—and drip on you, slide down to form pools on the groundsheet and also soak your sleeping bag wherever it touches the sides. This happens most towards the foot of the wedge-shaped tent because the space is so constructed around your feet. It also happens during rain showers when the tent door has to be closed.

Your body gives off water vapour to the equivalent of one pint of liquid a night, so there is no shortage of moisture to collect on tent walls which cannot 'breathe'.

So why not use materials which do breathe? Proofed cotton, for instance, which has been used for years as a tent material. The snag is when it rains. Whilst a proofed cotton tent is more robust than nylon, and allows the body warmth escape through the walls with little condensation, it will only keep out the rain because the threads in the weave swell and tighten when they become wet. This stops rain coming through, but it also means the water absorbed makes a wet cotton tent up to fifty per cent heavier.

Choose a lighter nylon tent then—but be ready for this fight against condensation. Check it is well ventilated with vents tailored into the design so that warm air is sucked outside. And know that other tips help: like always cooking outside the tent (as you did on the first night out); keeping a sponge nearby to mop down the walls—especially before going to sleep at night;

and storing wet clothing inside a plastic bag rather than in the
tent, the plastic bag then staying outside.

### It did rain, and the roof leaked

First, this is similar to when the topmost seam in a shop-bought
tent leaks from the beginning. Check this when you buy; that
all seams on your tent have been constructed to ensure
maximum watertightness.

Plastic—as nylon—may be completely waterproof, but if it
is not stretched glass-taut it can let water in. Water collects
along folds and wrinkles and can then drip through any tiny
punctures along such faults. Stretched out hard, however, the
plastic allows the rain to run off ducks-back fashion.

There is the additional point that nylon, like polythene, will
not shrink when wet—although cotton tents will. So all the
more need to pitch a tent made from synthetic material as taut
as possible.

### You scorched the tent and got wet cooking

This was a fault of the Hang Glider design (or did you forget to
check the weather forecast?). Lightweight tents do need a
porch over the entrance to allow you to cook outside the inner
tent yet still be protected directly above.

Without that porch . . . The clues are obvious. Rain was
sizzling off the hot lid on your pan, so you lifted the cooker
inside and a hot metal edge cut through the plastic (lucky for
you it wasn't an expensive nylon tent!), and the steam from the
pan condensed on the inner walls to drip all over you during the
process. If, however, you were frying food, then a different
kind of damage was possible—hot fat splattering the tent
fabric and sleeping bag, and so more damage done.

Do buy a tent with a porch, or resign yourself whenever it
rains to cooking in your anorak from the confines of your
sleeping bag as you lie half in and half out of the tent.

### The more you moved about trying to get to sleep the wetter you became . . .

This is the penalty of a nylon tent, and of one which suffers
poor ventilation. You have to restrict movement on lying down
or you rub against the condensation. Not that a single skin

cotton tent would be immune either—you have only to rub against these in the night and dew or rain on the outside will find their way inside as the weave opens under the pressure.

### It rained in the night and ran in on to the groundsheet

The penalty for not checking that weather forecast! This is another Hang Glider tent design fault. The water *can* swill inside if the ground outside becomes waterlogged. Modern tents, however, have what is termed a 'tray' or 'bathtub' floor which means the groundsheet is turned up at the edges to prevent water running in from the outside. (A snag here is that any water collecting here from condensation cannot run outside either—so a small sponge is handy).

### Your tent plastic was so taut it resembled solar panels glittering under the hot sun, and all your butter stowed inside melted on the blankets . . .

Not just a disadvantage of having a transparent tent, but of any single-skin tent. You feel the cold inside more AND the heat. It is the Timberline tent, however, which holds the answer here.

## TIMBERLINE TENT SYSTEMS FAILURES

The design of this shelter has several improvements, yet it is still lightweight and does not take up much room when packed. The flysheet (and its porch) inner tent which breathes, and A-pole, give you more space to move about inside and keep dry. The only snags are that separate groundsheet, and a flysheet which does not actually reach the ground. However, we now see how these affect your general performance.

### It began to drizzle as you pitched the tent, and the inner tent—not to mention YOU—became soaked

There was no need. You should have erected the flysheet first, then hung up the inner tent inside. Then you could have kept yourself and the inner tent under cover for most of the time. This, in fact, is a feature of most good modern tents as opposed to older-fashioned tents where you had to pitch the tent first before you could fit the flysheet. Look for it in the tent you eventually buy.

**The polythene flysheet and inner cotton tent were warmer during the night than your previous Hang Glider tent experience, but your autographed copy of** *Everest the Hard Way* **still got wet**

That's because you rightly took advantage of the storage space between flysheet and inner tent—but without stowing away those items into plastic bags first. The inner tent breathes. Fine, but the warm air inside still passes through to condense on the inside of the nylon—or, in your case, plastic—flysheet, and this trickles down on anything lying on the grass below . . .

**Your inner tent still let in water, however**

Two-skin tents you buy today have the outside of the inner tent lightly proofed so that this does not happen. This proofing in fact allows the moisture produced from your body to pass through and condense on the flysheet. This then drips back on to the inner tent, only the proofing on its outside prevents it from dripping back on to you. Your inner, however, had no such proofing and would let any drips from the flysheet through (though there should not have been too much dripping if in fact you did choose a fine warm night).

Another reason though for your getting wet could have been because you allowed the cotton inner tent and plastic flysheet to touch. And the point of contact, warmer inner against cool outer, produced drips. The inner tent and your flysheet must not be allowed to touch at any point, and a good lightweight tent will have this seperation incorporated in its design.

**Your inner ripped during pitching**

Good lightweight tents have guy and peg points reinforced on the inner tent and flysheet to prevent this happening. They are also carefully designed so the stress of tent pitching is taken by the seams and not by the cloth panels which clad the shelter—something you pay for instead of having just a large expanse of tent material as in the larger family-type multi-room tents.

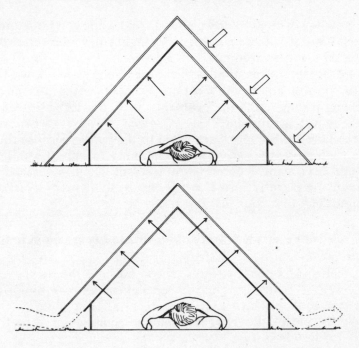

*Cavity Wall Tent Insulation*

## Your two-skinned tent was colder than the one-skin Hang Glider shelter

A layer of still air helps to prevent heat quickly escaping through it. Most houses sandwich air in between the bricks; for instance, cavity wall insulation. And windows sandwich air too when a layer of air is sealed between two layers of glass: double glazing. The same then goes for tents too. But only when the flysheet actually touches the ground all the way round, and so allows a layer of air to act as an insulator between the warm air in the tent and the cold air outside. When the flysheet does not touch the grass all the way round, the cold outer air then circulates inside it and over the inner tent so making it colder still inside.

The Timberline tent suffered from this design defect because it used up the plastic from your Hang Glider tent, and it was not quite big enough to go all round. And while you might not have noticed its effect on a warm dry night you would certainly do so on a cooler evening.

The lesson is a must: always choose a tent with a down-to-earth flysheet all the way round. Sometimes the ground is uneven, posing pitching problems with the down-to-earth flysheet just mentioned. This is solved, however, whenever those short rubber loops are fitted to the panels because they give each panel that amount of flexibility to self-adjust. The groundsheet being separate from the tent lets in a noticeable draught—especially after being in a tent with a fitted groundsheet like your last one.

**You needed kneepads after cooking on muddy grass out in the open**

You misunderstood. Always cook outside the tent, yes. However, in many instances when lightweight camping out you can cook beneath the flysheet entrance so long as the cooker is outside the inner tent, and is securely placed on the grass (of which more a little later).

**The tent poles broke**

It just goes to show . . . the strain of keeping a lightweight tent pitched is considerable, and is carried mainly by those specially designed seams *and* tent poles. No wonder they are often made from aircraft quality aluminium. Check any you buy are that good when they come with your new tent.

**It rained during the next morning and it was a hassle packing away inner tent, flysheet, groundsheet and string and skewers in the wet—not to mention how the soaking tentage then wet everything in your pack**

But you could have packed everything except the flysheet UNDER the flysheet; then rolled up and packed this last. Remember that the inner tent was only suspended on hooks and a couple of shoe laces. As for the dripping flysheet . . . an advantage of man-made fibres is they can be shaken hard and drops of moisture fly off to leave the material virtually dry again.

## MATTRESS PITFALLS YOU HAD TO TAKE LYING DOWN

It is a principle of lightweight camping that you lie in your sleeping bag and tent during anything but warm weather and cook in the doorway. It wasn't just a one-off experience for your two nights out. There are advantages to this—like keeping warm and rested after a possibly tiring day as you prepare your evening meal (or next morning's breakfast). It really is important, however, that you shield yourself from the ground as much as possible.

**The cold crept up through the blankets from below even though you padded the floor well for insulation**

The clue to your mistake here would be seen next morning in your once-fluffy 'mattress', by then reduced to a mushy pancake squashed flat. Not realising just how much cold can be lost to the ground—and nobody ever does until they go camping, even in the cold hours of a midsummer morning—you had chosen living foliage which contains juice. Crush these with your body weight and the insulation is lost. Instead, you need dead bracken, leaves, grass and so on which crackle like twigs and are full of 'dead air' spaces—so offering much improved insulation from the ground.

This kind of insulation is, in fact, rather similar in principle to the best you can buy: a bubble ground mat which by comparison to the mattress measures suggested so far is as effective as an electric blanket. Indeed, Scandinavians regularly use them instead of their traditional reindeer skin.

The bubble mat is a closed-cell foam mattress put under high pressure in an autoclave and pressurised with gas which permeates the material. On releasing the pressure the gas expands and creates thousands of closed-cell bubbles in the foam which is the secret of good insulation.

**The fitted groundsheet of the Hang Glider tent proved messy**

Condensation pooled on it as it could not escape. And when you wrapped the tent away, the underside of the groundsheet was covered with mud, bits of grass and worm casts—muckier than wrapping up the separate groundsheet of the Timberline tent. Remedy: a small sponge will mop up any spillage, and wipe down the bottom of the groundsheet before packing away. Also, as we see later, it is often a good idea to place an insulating pad under the groundsheet in the first instance.

**You borrowed an airbed, but found it rock hard and, on a cold night, chilly**

Airbeds should not be blown up too hard—only a thirdful of air is needed. But they are still too cold. It is like sleeping on a cold hot water bottle!

## SLEEPING BAG BLUES

It is difficult to overestimate the importance of a really good sleeping bag—living in it as you will be for some daylit hours as well as darkness during your excursions. Quality is only achieved at a fairly high cost, however.

Both sleeping bags you made worked, but posed problems perhaps. Good: all the more strength to your critical powers when you go to buy one. Here we are concerned with how they are made, however. In the next chapter details are given on the appropriate fillings other than hay, but for now let's see how the bag you may end up buying is made. Fault-finding in a home-made bag makes you appreciate the vital points even more.

**Both blanket and paper bags were difficult to pack**

A reason why good sleeping bags are expensive is because their fillings allow them to be compressed into a really small space. The cheaper the sleeping bag, the more bulky it is likely to be to stow away. But as your two bags have been made virtually for nothing, what can you expect?

There is another point concerning the Hayloft bag, though. You may have stuffed too much hay into it. It's an understandable belief that the more 'loft' in a bag (its thickness when fluffed out, in fact) the warmer the bag will be. But it is misleading. There are other factors which affect a sleeping bag's performance. The shape of the bag, for instance. The way it is stitched; its exposure to wind and damp; the physical condition, metabolism and thickness of clothing of the person inside it. And even the shape of your tent can affect sleeping bag insulation.

### The bags you made fell to bits

They must have been badly made. The blanket bedroll secured with big safety pins through each thickness will normally hold. So will the brown paper sleeping bag when made with care.

It's the same with shop-bought sleeping bags. If they are made by a reputable firm, you should have little to worry about. However, a cheap sleeping bag could well have the stitching that drifts apart and allows the filling to wander from the original pockets inside—not to mention letting it spill out on occasion. There is more in the next chapter on picking out the winners. Enough to say now that one of the marks of quality—and there are a number of others—is when a cotton thread with a nylon core is used; the nylon gives strength and the cotton expands when wet, filling the stitch holes and making it more water resistant.

### The Hayloft bag became wet during the night

Never let your sleeping bag get wet. This is why the paper sleeping bag was introduced only at the Timberline tent stage—so you could use it with a dry cotton inner tent. You should always carry your sleeping bag in its own 'stuff' sack—the bag in which it comes already stuffed—AND a plastic bag around. Then you need to unfurl it inside the already pitched tent.

The reason is that not even the best sleeping bags are waterproof. Nylon and cotton are the two most commonly used 'shell' materials; nylon being lighter while cotton is more comfortable. Some bags have a cotton inner and nylon outer, for instance. This shell material, however, is only partly water repellent (but not waterproof) because it is necessary for the body moisture to escape and waterproofing would cause the moisture to condense inside the bag—making the user wet and damaging the filling.

### The Klondyke bedroll felt cold

Even with a cellular blanket sandwiched between two wool blankets as suggested, it was still chilly . . . The fault would then be found in anything which interfered with the sleeping bag's role of keeping out cold and damp, while holding in the warmth generated by your body.

It might have been gaps between the blankets where you pinned them. Or it was a colder night than you bargained for, and you were a blanket short of what was really needed. Perhaps you lacked sufficient insulation below you. Also your straight and rectangular-shaped bedroll—as is the Klondyke shape—tends to leave more room around the feet and shoulders and can prove colder because of this than a tapered bag like the Hayloft.

### But there were cold areas in the Hayloft bag

Your quilt construction methods probably slipped. And it's not really your fault either, because sellotape could have peeled away from the brown paper when you rolled up the bag. Wherever a pocket of hay may have come adrift you would feel a 'cold spot'—something quite common in the cheaper bags.

Or did you perhaps decide to use just simple quilting—as shown—and think that would be enough? This is the least effective of sleeping bag designs because there are then cold spots at all the seams. Just what you might expect from a cheap bag, without overlapping pockets of filling.

Your double quilting was simply this: quilted pockets with seams overlapping to stop those cold spots, etc. It is a simple way of boosting insulation; however it doubles the weight of the shell material and—as you found—it IS hard to pack.

There are three other designs, though, where the sleeping bag fillings are separated by baffles—fabric walls which stop the filling from circulating from one section to another: box wall baffles; slant baffles; and V-baffles, the last two being found in better quality bags. The illustration gives the idea, and you should always check just what kind of baffles are used in the bag you buy.

### The Hayloft bag had two cold spots right down the sides

The two seams where back and front panel meet were to blame; almost as if they were metal zip fasteners, in fact. On a warm night you would not notice, but once it turned cold you felt it

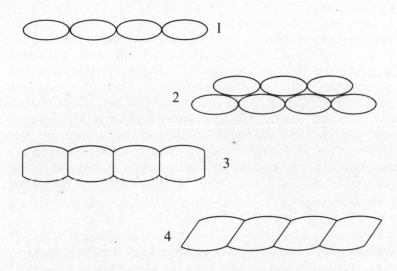

*How a Sleeping Bag Can Baffle You*
*1. Stitched Through Quilting   2. Double Quilting Construction*
*3. Wall Quilting   4. Slant Wall Baffle Construction*

immediately in these places. So avoid bags which are zipped in this way. They will always have cold spots unless the zips are padded over with quilted flaps. Even then they are unnecessary for lightweight camping.

### The Hayloft bag became too warm

Not with a corner catching fire as you cooked I hope! (Cooking was banned for the night you used this brown paper sleeping bag!) However, if you also wore clothes inside it on a warm night—no wonder. The tapered shape bag is always warmer for a start. And here its filling is so effective it can even cook meals on its own . . . Well, of course, you found it warm. It is exactly the same with a good sleeping bag. On summer evenings it might prove too hot even when sleeping with no clothes on. But you can always pull the top part down, like socks in summer.

And this inconvenience is as nothing during cold spells when the warm filling of hay really pays off.

'Hey,' you say. 'How can hay cook supper on its own?' Well, not quite on its own, is the answer. But almost. Here's how. Take a cardboard box and pack the bottom tightly with hay. Now stand a cooking pot inside it and pack all around this container with more tightly-stuffed hay. Then fill a bag with more hay which will fit the top of the box (and cover the pot's lid). Now take out the pot, fill it with minced beef, sliced onion, salt, potatoes and carrots etc. Bring it to the boil on your kitchen stove and simmer for ten minutes or so. Then replace the pot into the hole in the hay, cover it with the hay bag on top (weighted with a stone) and so good are the insulating properties of the hay your meal will be kept simmering until you eat it, say, the following evening.

**Both Klondyke and Hayloft sleeping bags were too small**

Buy a full-size sleeping bag, however old or big you are now. Then you won't need another as you grow older or bigger. Fold the end of the bag over if it is too long now—as you did in the first place with the Klondyke.

## CAMP COOKING HASSLES

'Buy a stove instead of an axe' is advice given to young American backpackers today—on ecological grounds as well as safety ones. You then keep the wilds as natural as possible, as there is no chopping off boughs or otherwise butchering trees for bonfire fuel. And if you are ever in a jam you can always brew up a mug of tea to fortify yourself . . . How right this is.

Cooking on a wood fire is fine, but often impractical when camping on the move. It is hard to light when raining, impossible on high ground where there are few trees, and impractical to kindle just outside the tent door. Your little cooker, however, will produce a relatively slow, controlled heat, while a fire takes too long to warm up, tends to become too hot and takes a long while to cool down. It could take minutes or as much as hours to cook a meal properly on a fire; you need to keep stirring all the time. Not that camp stoves provide no problems, but then much depends on the kind of stove you eventually buy. As to this, your small candle powered burner gives examples good and bad.

### The cooking took too long

You have a choice of five kinds of shop-bought stove: paraffin, petrol, meths, solid fuel and camping gas (butane). Under certain conditions all of these can also prove slow burners. Solid fuel stoves, for instance, which are fine for weekend bivouacs, can still seem lazy when you need them urgently. Camping gas must be kept above freezing or it just doesn't work. Meths stoves can be seen to burn at a crawl, especially in calm conditions. And petrol and paraffin stoves are affected by really cold conditions too. Don't expect wonders from a small stove therefore; yet it's not as though you need sit out in the open when cooking. And, as we see, there are ways of speeding up cooking on such a small heat source.

### The cooker's flame sooted up the pots

Carry cooking utensils in a plastic bag always.

### The tent walls became spattered with cooking fat

You must have been cooking too near the tent doorway with the kind of food not recommended at this kind of proximity to your tent (even if it is blowing a gale): such as bacon. Flying fat will damage costly tent fabrics. As an alternative to bacon and egg for breakfast, what's wrong instead with, say, porridge and a couple of hard boiled eggs?

### The stove tipped over

Small cookers are bound to be unstable. Some have legs which can be pushed into the ground, but even these need buttressing in wind with tent pegs as shown. Only then are they more solid. And always remember that earlier tip about locking your stove to the ground by surrounding its base with tent pegs or meat skewers pushed into the ground. These should press round it tightly from all quarters.

### Wind affected the cooker's flame

A strong draught will make a meths cooker burn all the better, but it can affect paraffin and petrol stoves the other way

too—especially when trying to start them. You need a separate
windshield for the cooker you buy—as well as a big rock to
reinforce this cover.

### You took a frying pan; it wasn't necessary

It's up to you. Food for this kind of lightweight camping
should be kept dead simple. Many such meals can be prepared
in one pot or pan—by a system we see later in Chapter 6—so
you can take along the very minimum of utensils and yet cook
the food you like. A frying pan does tend to produce meals
the hard way.

### You scalded a finger

It could happen with any small cooker if you forgot a basic
rule: always hold the pan you are stirring with the other hand.
And whenever doing anything to your stove remove the pot or
pan on top.

### You burned your lips

Another rule you overlooked. Forget tin mugs, plates and
bowls. And plastic ones that can bend. Test them at home first.

## SUMMARY

You have now experienced two nights' camping and, I hope, a
lot of fun—if only looking back on this chapter of accidents.
Go over the pros and cons of the simple equipment you used,
and start deciding what you must buy first. The next chapter
will help; the rest is your decision. A single-skinned tent which
does sweat is, for instance, quite in order, if you have been
loaned one, and as long as you know what you are letting
yourself in for—namely, condensation. So you are prepared to
take the preventive steps against such trouble? Great! . . . With
this state of mind you should have every chance of success,
expecially as you are only likely to be using it during summer
months at first anyway.

This two nights' programme carried out systematically
should also have shown you the need for those systems
(remember?) which develop from the particular gear you buy.

# 4 Equipment

You need two kinds of camping kit: equipment accommodating you away from home, and the means of carrying it. In some cases things overlap; you might, for example, have some of the transportation gear already. If you plan a holiday camping by roads or rivers, for instance, you will probably already have the cycle you pedal or the canoe you paddle. Go backpacking, however, and you might have to buy boots, rucksack and weatherproof clothing as well—it's that kind of adventure where people can start from impulse more easily because the activity involved is simply walking across country from one camp site to the next. But you need the gear.

Let's look at actual camping gear first, then the means by which you carry it and other accessories required.

## HOW TO CUT EQUIPMENT COSTS

Where will you use your equipment? Is the tent intended for sheltered lowland sites, for instance, or is more rugged country with little natural protection from the elements your aim—like moorland or seashore? Will the tent be used as a base camp so that it stands on one site for several days while you walk, climb, swim, fish or whatever, only returning to it at night? Or will you carry tent and supplies with you each day as you tour from camp site to camp site? Will the tent be used only by you or will you share it with a friend? All these factors must be considered first as they must influence your choice.

Tents and sleeping bags can be divided very generally into valley and mountain designs. Naturally a valley tent will cost less than the more robust mountain shelter. And for most young people the valley tent will be fine. Camping on mountains is something else and as I stressed in my book,

*Climbing for Young People*, there is danger involved. Camping high means you should first have the experience of walks and climbs done in all conditions, and if you really do have this, then buy a mountain tent. If not, however, set your sights lower for now.

Try to obtain the widest view of camping gear first so you can decide better what you want. It pays to shop around the big outdoor stores (and small ones too) as prices for identical items can vary a great deal. Visit your nearest outdoor shop in the first instance, and ask about tents, sleeping bags and stoves. Also ask for catalogues and price lists. You can also obtain these by post from the many manufacturers who advertise in magazines like *Climber & Rambler, The Great Outdoors, Camping* and *Practical Camper.*

Some stockists, furthermore, produce catalogues which are in effect handbooks full of hints, tips, advice and suggestions on exactly how to get the best from the equipment listed. You can't go wrong with names like: *Pindisports, Alpine Sports, YHA, Field and Trek, Blacks, Benjamin Edgington, Frank Davies, Brighams, Joe Brown, The Practical Camper, Graham Tiso, Nevisport* and *Robert Lawrie* to mention a few such stores.

Second-hand bargains are advertised in camping and other outdoor magazines—not to mention *Exchange & Mart*. But only buy by mail order if you can first obtain the goods on approval. There is so much that could be wrong with them now.

## THE PICK AND CHOOSE SYSTEM

When it comes to buying equipment . . . aim to buy everything from one good specialist shop (like the ones mentioned above). If there are several of you buying together, ask for discount. And don't panic when you see the prices. Acquiring all your kit can take several years: you build it up gradually, using a system of 'pick and choose'. It's a good idea.

Pick all the items which are marginally necessary from inexpensive sources, but carefully choose items like tent, sleeping bag and stove which are essential for comfort and safety. The result—if you think it out—will be a good outfit, suitable for a wide range of outdoor trips and for all but the most severe conditions. The key to making good equipment choices is to spend money only on the things you really need—rather than on luxuries and gimmicks which swallow up your camping pounds and pence. Done this way, and with help from your friends when you share the cost, you will find it less costly than you first thought.

Motivation in camping is important, and the fact you have bought a tent can give you the drive to making-do for the time being with other improvised items. For instance, you may not now be able to afford a sleeping bag and Optimus stove, but on the other hand you don't really need to—especially in summer. Camping trips should be kept short at first, and only undertaken in countryside that is not too remote. And you can use blankets and a cheap solid fuel stove to go with your brand-new shelter which will actually then give the 'pride of ownership' feeling (corny-sounding, but it works) to use this improvised tackle with some purpose. It's the same idea as using a new cricket bat you have bought for a game with an old ball and sticks for wickets. You get more out of it because you have invested in it, even if only one piece of kit at a time.

THE CHART ON THE FOLLOWING PAGES GIVES EXAMPLES OF THIS—SHOWING YOU HOW TO SAVE COSTS YET ACCUMU-LATE YOUR EQUIPMENT AT THE SAME TIME IN THIS VERY WAY.

| PURSUIT | TENT | SLEEPING BAG & INSULATING PAD | STOVE |
|---|---|---|---|
| BACKPACKING | In winter, when the backpacking season begins, a double-skinned tent is a must (with fly, porch and fitted groundsheet). In summer, however, just a flysheet can be used. OR a cheap two-skin tent made in Japan or Taiwan will serve as well, but with some reservations for rugged winter use. | A bag filled with duck or goose down is best for serious backpacking. However, *a good synthetic-filled bag runs it a close second, and will be cheaper though rather heavier and bulkier.* A closed-cell foam mat is also needed. | An Optimus paraffin stove OR meths storm cooker is a vital aid in winter. In summer, though, a cheap solid fuel stove would do at first, like a Meta picnic cooker. |
| POTHOLING & CAVING | A good two-skinned tent is needed for surviving wild moorland after travelling through underground. | *A synthetic bag (a good one) could be great here*: the alternative is a good down bag. | An Optimus paraffin or meths stove are essential. |

CANOEING

A cheap two-skin tent made in Japan or Taiwan would be OK here. For winter paddling however, a better class of two-skin tent would be advised.

A good synthetic-filled bag will protect you even if it falls into the water; it will dry quickly when wrung out and hung in the sun. However, *a cheaper way is to make a Klondyke bedroll from blankets and stitch them in place (this will do less damage than pinning them together) with strong thread and big simple stitches. Although it is bulky you should be able to find room for the bedroll in your craft if a proper bag is too expensive.*

(continued in next column)

*A cheap solid fuel stove will do at first to save cost*—but chew carbohydrates (sweets, for instance) during the day to keep your energy going.

*A barely inflated life jacket will cushion the hips plus the turf, heather, hay alternative described on page 50 will do as insulating pad at first.*

| PURSUIT | TENT | SLEEPING BAG & INSULATING PAD | STOVE |
|---------|------|------------------------------|-------|
| ORIENTEERING | A cheap two-skin tent is fine at first, but a better quality shelter is needed in really wild country and against keen competition. | *The Klondyke bedroll is usable here as you can arrive at the orienteering site by car,* and therefore bulk in transit is no problem. Otherwise a synthetic-filled bag is a good choice. | An Optimus paraffin or meths storm cooker is needed due to the element of urgency involved in the contest— and you don't know when it might overlap with your camping needs. |
| ROCK CLIMBING | A cheap two-skin Japanese or Taiwan-made tent is valid for mountain base camps on the valley floor. And in the hands of experienced climbers might be used quite high on hills too—but it does need that experience. | A down-filled bag goes with climbing of any sort as it packs away so small and is very warm. And one day, though you may be camping at a low-level now, you might be bivouacking high when you really need it. A closed-cell foam pad is another must. | Use an Optimus paraffin stove from the start. OR the meths storm cooker. |

MOUNTAINEERING

A two-skinned quality mountain tent is the only answer for sleeping high. Flysheet, porch and fitted groundsheet are necessary. Probably A-poles too (perhaps slid down sleeves in the tent panels) and possibly with a sleeve entrance at one end and zipped door at the other.

(The ideal combination again would be, if you can afford it, to camp beneath the flysheet on valley bottom sites and the fully rigged tent on the actual mountains.)

A good down-filled bag and insulating pad are musts.

An Optimus paraffin or meths storm cooker.

| PURSUIT | TENT | SLEEPING BAG & INSULATING PAD | STOVE |
|---|---|---|---|
| CYCLING | A cheap two-skin tent made in Japan or Taiwan will be fine here—possibly just the flysheet in summer. | A good synthetic-filled bag would be cheaper than a down-filling here; but buy one that is under 4lbs in weight. Hay, heather, or springy turf with that spare inner-tube a third full of air below your hips can be your sleeping pad at first. | A cheap solid fuel stove will do for summer, but use a primus or meths storm cooker in winter. |
| SNORKELLING | A cheap two-skinned tent would do in summer. | The Klondyke bedroll would work well too in summer as you will often arrive by car or motor cycle. An insulating pad of heather, dried ferns etc would be a cost-saver too. | Cheap solid fuel stove OK. |

# BUYING YOUR FIRST TENT

Tents come in all sizes and shapes of the geometrical textbook: wedges, triangles, rectangles, squares, rhomboids and even circles. They all serve different purposes, some better than others and depending on what you want. The single pole tent, for instance, will offer lots of room—especially when it hangs from an A-pole on the outside so there is no centre pole inside. This means it is high in the centre so you can stand up inside it. Equipped with fitted groundsheet and a flysheet with porch it is indeed luxurious accommodation in the wigwam style. However, such tents tend to be heavier and more expensive than the two-pole design you have already experienced with your Timberline tent. They are not so streamlined either, and do not withstand strong winds as well.

The two-pole tent is the one for you now. It may come with orthodox tent poles or A-poles, or a form of A-pole which is actually more of an archway shaped like an upside down 'U' than an 'A'. But generally it will prove best for your purposes as there are now so many designs on the market to this general pattern.

Costly as such tents are—between £20 and £90—you will find sharing a tent immediately halves and can even cut costs by a third. However much of a loner you may be, and hankering to go it alone, this is simply not safe when you are still young. You must most definitely go with others, and sharing a tent is an essential part of your safety precautions. Indeed, it is only common sense. Can you imagine four people on a backpacking, canoeing or cycling trip carrying a tent each? Instead, four people would best camp in pairs under two tents while a three-man group could use one shelter when everything is planned that way first and provision duly made.

So buy a two-man tent rather than a one-man. Come the time when you may be using it on your own, at least you will have gained experience by then. And you will certainly have room to be comfortable. But a three-man shelter! How can you convert a two-man tent to this? Quite easily when you use A-poles to create more space inside. Although A-poles will add a pound or two in weight and cost extra, they are worth it when you think an extra person can be sheltered for this relatively

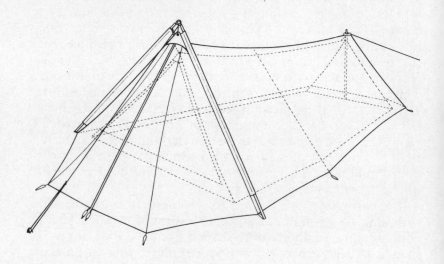

*The Ultimate Tramp*

small price. (Incidentally, proper A-poles are not quite like those used to support your Timberline tent as they actually straddle the tent panels which are suspended from and between them.)

Good tents are made by *Vango, Bukta, Ultimate, Blacks, Merrill, Edgington, Robert Saunders* and *Fjallraven*—to mention some. Go for these when choosing your tent. However good the make, though, ask to see your tent pitched first; then crawl inside and examine it.

A good modern lightweight tent should be roomy yet snug. . . . And draught-proof but well-ventilated, capable of being pitched quickly (and also of being taken down speedily) yet be as buoyant when pitched as a stunter kite. Such a well-made tent will have rotproof, windproof and water repellent fabrics (even inner tents which breathe should have a light waterproof coating to delay moisture seeping through from the outside); tent poles of strong light aluminium; seams stitched in the fabric by special watertight processes so water cannot leak through the holes; strong rubber loops around the base of the flysheet so the panels are kept taut even on uneven ground; air vents which allow warm air to be sucked out of the tent; and door zips which close from bottom to top so you can still ventilate the tent through the top of the door left open. Besides these features, the tent will also incorporate improvements you know from experience in the Hang Glider and Timberline tents are 'musts'—like a flysheet which actually touches the ground, and bell ends which wrap the tent at front and back in flysheet protection as well as along the sides.

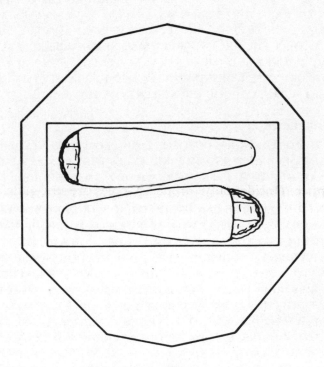

*The Ultimate 'High Country 2'*

### The best buy if you can afford it . . .

BUY A DOUBLE-SKINNED TENT THAT WEIGHS LESS THAN 5½lbs. IT SHOULD HAVE FITTED GROUNDSHEET, BREATHABLE INNER TENT AND NYLON FLYSHEET WITH PORCH. THE DESIGN SHOULD ALLOW THE FLYSHEET TO BE PITCHED FIRST, THEN THE INNER INSIDE IT. THE FLYSHEET IN FACT CAN THEN BE USED AS A TENT ON ITS OWN DURING WARM WEATHER. (PLEASE NOTE: A LIGHT TENT WILL BE OBVIOUSLY EASIER TO CARRY ON A LONG TRIP WHERE EVERY KILOGRAM SAVED WILL BE GRATEFULLY FELT. HOWEVER, THE LIGHTER THE TENT THE MORE IT WILL COST.)

### The second-best buy . . .

IF A GOOD QUALITY DOUBLE-SKIN TENT IS TOO EXPENSIVE, THEN YOU MAY BE ABLE TO AFFORD A CHEAP TWO-SKIN TENT MADE IN JAPAN OR TAIWAN AND SOLD IN MANY HIGH STREET CAMPING AND GENERAL STORES SUCH AS ARMY & NAVY, PETERS AND MILLETS. SUCH TENTS ARE STILL SERVICEABLE AND THE ONLY SNAG IS THAT THE GROUNDSHEET MAY NEED TO BE REPLACED FAIRLY QUICKLY AND THE GENERAL MATERIALS WILL NOT BE AS ROBUST OR AS WELL DESIGNED AS IN A GOOD QUALITY TENT. YOU CAN BUY A PRETTY GOOD CHEAP TENT FOR £20–£30.

### The third choice . . .

BUYING A ONE-SKIN NYLON TENT, EVEN FROM A GOOD FIRM, IS NOT RECOMMENDED. IN SOME INSTANCES THEY CAN ACTUALLY COST AS MUCH OR EVEN MORE THAN A TWO-SKIN SHELTER. HOWEVER, IF YOU HAVE BEEN GIVEN OR PRESENTED WITH A ONE SKIN NYLON TENT YOU CAN USE IT FOR NOW, ONLY DO BE AWARE OF THE CONDENSATION IT WILL PRODUCE ON ITS INSIDE WALLS AND TRY NOT TO RUB AGAINST THE INSIDES. YOU WILL FIND IT IS QUITE A PROBLEM TOO! HOWEVER, CONDENSATION CAN BE KEPT DOWN TO SOME EXTENT IF THE FOLLOWING PREVENTIVE MEASURES ARE TAKEN: SLEEP WITH YOUR HEAD DIRECTLY BENEATH THE GAUZE PANEL UNDER ONE OF THE EAVES SO YOUR HOT BREATH IS DRAWN OUT OF THE TENT; NEVER COOK INSIDE THE TENT BUT INSTEAD PEG OUT THE DOOR AND COOK JUST OUTSIDE SO ALL THE STEAM GOES OUT INTO THE AIR; KEEP ALL WET CLOTHING INSIDE A POLYTHENE BAG; AND ALWAYS HAVE A SPONGE HANDY FOR OCCASIONAL MOPPING DOWN OF DROPS OF CONDENSATION APPEARING ON THE TENT WALLS.

## YOUR SLEEPING BAG

The kind you buy will depend on how much you can afford. Try not to pinch pennies, however. A good sleeping bag will last a lifetime and pay many times over in the comfort it gives.

What the bag is filled with is most important. Hay was fine for one night, but something more durable is needed for permanent use. There are two kinds of such filling: 1) down—the light fluffy cluster containing no stalk or quill found on the underside of ducks and geese, and 2) man-made fibres.

A down-filled bag will certainly be the warmest and also roll up smaller than one filled with synthetic fibres. It will also be lighter. A sleeping bag should not weigh more than 4lbs at the most if you intend backpacking (and most bags under this

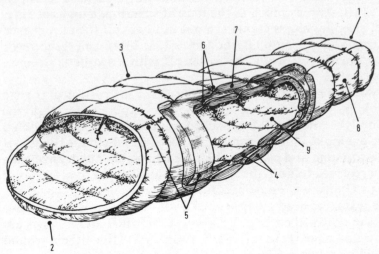

*The Ultimate Forty Wink Sleeping Bag*
*1. Box foot   2. Shaped hood with drawcords*
*3. Contoured body Shape   4. Double quilt Construction*
*5. Offset seams   6. Offset quilting*
*7. Continuous filament polyester fibre stitched in place so will not move in baffles   8. Ripstop nylon outer*
*9. Comfortable Polyester cotton lining*

weight are down-filled). Yet you will be able to roll up such a bag again and again without the filling 'matting' together. A light shaking is all you need do to bring back a good down-filled bag to its original expanded condition before you climb inside.

This only applies when the down is dry, however. Once it becomes wet through condensation, say, or it falls into water, its insulating properties are lost. The feathers stick together and lose their precious 'loft'.

And synthetic materials? The best are polyester fibres like Dacron Fibrefill II and P3 (as some big stores have used in Continental quilts for several years with great success) and they are not as expensive. Buy a warm bag containing such a filling, but don't expect it to pack away into the same small space as a down bag. However, it will have one big advantage: it will not attract or absorb moisture. Even when soaked it will still work. You can wring it out, climb inside and still be warm. It also dries out fast. And as much as the idea of spending a night out in a wet sleeping bag is enough to put mothers off the idea of ever letting you go camping, the fact is that if the emergency ever happened—you would be better off with a synthetic sleeping bag.

After checking the filling, go over the construction of the bag looking for the same points you experienced with the Klondyke and Hayloft models. Examine the kind of quilting, for example, and the general finish of the shell: the quality of the stitching and cut, and the type of baffles which have been interspersed to keep the filling apart inside. The final factors in your choice will come back to cost and weight. Backpackers, for instance, need a bag around 3½lbs heavy, still the preserve of the down-filled bag. Yet some Fibrefill II and P3 bags are now down nearly to this mark, and you will find others around the 4lbs range.

## THAT MATTRESS

A closed-cell foam mat is invaluable, and the only excuse for not taking one with you on a camping trip is that you might just not have the space. And if you are camping in an area where there will be plenty of natural bedding like turf, straw, hay or heather anyway, you can temporarily substitute with these.

# THE YOUNG PERSON'S STOVE

The few light meals cooked on your candle burner so far will have shown you one thing. How much easier it is to fall asleep feeling warm and well-fed. That you continued to sleep well with the warmth glowing through you as the hot food was digested, and then woke next morning to be refreshed by more hot coffee and porridge, cooked easily at arm's length from your sleeping bag, is a great feeling. And only a few cooking utensils were needed, not least of these being the stove.

There are five types of camping stove: solid fuel, meths, paraffin, petrol and camping gas. Of these the petrol stove uses an expensive fuel and can be risky to run; the solid fuel stove is convenient but is not a speedy source if you need hot food urgently; the gas stove is even more convenient but it is the most costly in its fuel; the meths stove can prove a slow burner and is thirsty on its quite expensive fuel; and the Primus uses a good economic fuel but is mechanically more demanding.

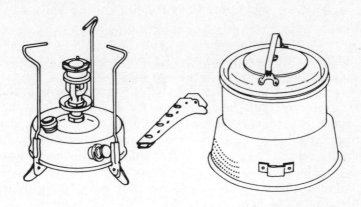

*The Young Person's Stove*

It is the Optimus paraffin stove (the original in fact), which remains the most popular stove because it is safe, efficient, cheaply-fuelled and powerful: the half-pint version, for instance, gives you two hours of cooking time on one filling and will boil a quart of water in less than 5 minutes. These stoves still burn well in sub-zero temperatures, at high altitudes, and in very windy conditions. It was Optimus who also made the original Svea paraffin stoves, too—still available today. Details of how to operate this stove are given in Chapter 6; just remember now that however readily paraffin is available as fuel, this stove needs priming to get it to go. In an emergency this can be done with paraffin, but normally you would use meths or solid fuel tablets broken into pieces. Of these, solid fuel, is the better of the two. It does mean you need to carry two fuels for your stove, however. Optimus also make a burning paste which you squeeze from a tube.

The alternative choice of stove is the meths storm cooker made by Trangia Fjallraven or Optimus (73A model). It lives up to its name (you can still cook in a wind), is safe and you buy a good set of pots with it, everything fitting together as a unit. It is certainly one of the most stable cookers available as it has a potstand which surrounds both the pot on the boil and the burner.

*Some more points to note.* The ideal group for young campers is four, and this is best served by one cooker to each pair of campers: you can have two pots cooking at the same time, important in bad weather when warm food is a must. Make sure too you have the correct fuel. Accidents have happened where mistakes have been made. It is the main reason certainly why petrol stoves are not recommended, generally safe as they are. It is just that they pose additional risks. Lastly, bottle your paraffin or meths by the pint in a Sigg aluminium bottle or improvise for now with strong plastic bottles that have held soft drinks.

## COOKING UTENSILS

You need: KFS, mug, deep plate or bowl (unbreakable, but not aluminium, as it is too hot to hold with hot food inside it), waterbag or plastic bottle and pots and pans which are light and which pack into a really small space. These come with the meths storm stoves mentioned, but with an Optimus you will have to buy your own. Nesting billy cans are easy to pack and save space, but buy only a simple canteen set. This will consist of a pot that holds a pint and has a lid which can double as a frying pan (and act as a plate-and-mixing bowl, too). Then fit a smaller pot inside to make a pair. Pots with a rolled rim round the top are easier to pick up and put down with your last item: a Bulldog pan grabber.

## FOOD

You need enough food for each day of your camping excursion and, just as important, it should be the kind of food you like to eat. Calculate that you will eat around 2lbs of food a day, say, 5lbs for a weekend. And then make your choice. The best system for this, as we see later, is that you eat a quick breakfast, then forget your actual lunch as such but instead chew sweets, raisins, chocolate, dried fruit, Kendal mint cake or other energy-boosting foods through the day. Then, after pitching camp, you cook a hot meal for supper.

Choose food that is easy to cook and light to carry like dried vegetables, mashed potato and dehydrated soups and curries (and even omelettes!). Forget about tins for now as they are heavy to carry, and contain liquids which have to be poured away—except, of course, your favourite cans of baked beans. Meat can be bought from the butchers—in which case you will need to eat it the same, or possibly the next, day while it is fresh. Or you can buy the plastic packets of it—mentioned in Chapter 2—which you cook inside the packet in boiling water. Luncheon meat and corned beef in tins is another choice. It really does depend on what you like best; the kind of stuff you would in fact eat at home. Eggs, for instance, can be carried safely in plastic boxes, or stored already broken in air-tight containers. Jam, marmalade, condensed milk, meat and vegetable pastes can be bought in tubes and keep their flavour to the last squeeze. And other forms of condensed food which take up the least space are: dried soup, rice, macaroni, porridge oats, muesli, milk powder, dehydrated fruit juice, hard tack biscuits, Ryvita, cream crackers and powdered drinks. You can buy them all at supermarkets, although you may need to split the packets down into smaller packages for your trips before setting out.

## THE EQUIPMENT YOU NEED FOR CARRYING CAMPING KIT

Walking, cycling and canoeing are the most popular ways of travelling with a tent, and being completely self-sufficient. Here are the details of the basic things you need for such exciting tours (useful addresses on page 100).

## ALL YOU NEED TO GO BACKPACKING

The idea is to carry tent, sleeping bag etc in a rucksack from one camp site to the next, walking the distances in between. Backpackers should not be confused with less independent types. Unlike campers or mere hikers, they carry everything they need to survive at least a long weekend in the wilds. Properly equipped with enough food and drink and the right weatherproof clothing they can safely penetrate our most remote and rugged regions. But wait! Before you stride out into the unknown, remember that what you are about to do is potentially dangerous. You can only be safe with careful planning, and the right equipment.

### Boots

Soles should be flexible and thick enough to shock-absorb your feet from stones, and they should have cleated rubber Vibram treads. Other essentials are: one-piece leather uppers, bellows tongue, D-rings and hooks for the laces and padding inside. The most important requirement is comfort, so buy only from a specialist outdoor shop.

### Clothing

Several thin layers of clothing are much better than one thick one. This is because they trap several layers of air to keep you warm. But they are also more comfortable. If you are wearing several thin sweaters it is easy to take one off if you feel too hot. And if you get wet it's a lot easier to dry several thin layers than one thick one. A long-sleeved shirt and thin wool sweaters are the ideal then, but what you wear next to the skin should be what you feel best in. It might be a string vest or a wool vest or a cotton tee-shirt. The main thing is you should feel comfortable in it. What to wear on top of everything as a 'shell', however, is something else. The old problem of finding something to wear on top which will keep out rain, wind and snow, but will not also trap condensation inside (as with your tent!), has been solved. The riddle-breaker is a new material called Goretex. Trap it over a cup of hot coffee with a rubber band and steam rises through; turn the cup upside down and the coffee will not leak. It breathes! The only snag, however, is the cost. A Goretex jacket costs three times as much as one made from proofed nylon. And Goretex tents—still being tested at the time of writing this—will also be very expensive.

You will also need a balaclava or woollen cap which, when pulled down over the ears, prevents nearly a quarter of your body heat escaping from the top of the head; a pair of mitts to prevent frost nipping fingers; long woollen socks; and long zip-up gaiters to keep small stones, water and snow out of your boots.

Always take a set of spare clothes with you so you have a complete change of dry things whenever you get wet. It's a vital safety rule.

### Rucksack

Pack frames are the Red Indian way of carrying the sack strapped to a frame which is then slung high on the shoulders. They are certainly the best way of carrying heavy loads except that young people should never carry more for comfort and safety than the number of years in their age. If you are 12, say, you carry a small rucksack carrying just that: 12lbs. In which case a small climber's 'day sack' is ideal for you—simply a waterproof bag with well-padded shoulder straps and a big flap on top to keep the rain out.

Older young people, however, need a pack frame or—and the trend is towards this type—an anatomically shaped rucksack with a light, flexible internal frame. It is in fact a larger kind of day sack, described above, but designed so that it just seems to float along high on your shoulders. Sometimes there are side pockets in which you can store things like stove and fuel bottle; in other designs there are no outer attachments

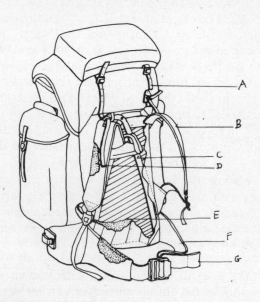

*An Exploded Anatomical Rucksack (The Cyclops Echo)*
*A. Adjustable tensioners    B. Padded Shoulder straps*
*C. Adjustable internal alloy frame    D. Closed cell foam padding*
*E. Canvas Back    F. Padded hip fins    G. Quick release Bergbuckle*

whatever except straps and buckles for an ice axe, and yet you quickly discover the best way of fitting all your possessions inside. The base of the sack might well be reinforced in leather or double layers of nylon while the top flap could well have a zipped compartment in which to keep camera, coins, matches, and other small and readily-needed items.

Never buy a pack frame or rucksack without a padded waist belt. This transfers much of the load from the shoulders to the strong bones of your pelvis via the hips. It also pays to buy only from a specialist outdoor shop as fitting the right-sized pack for your shape and size can take as much as half an hour.

## Lighting

Take a flashlight on an elastic headband; spare battery and bulbs; and long-life camping candles (or ordinary candles failing these).

## Fibre-pile suit

Helly Hansen top and trousers make ideal pyjamas, but your pyjamas will probably be adequate. The fur-like inners (of the fibre-pile garments) make excellent outdoor underwear and keep warm even when damp.

## Map and compass

Ordnance Survey 1:50,000 sheets and a Silva compass are 'musts'.

## Whistle

This is for emergencies. Choose a plastic one that won't freeze to the lips.

## Plastic bags and newspapers

Polythene bags have many uses—especially for storing wet clothing, food and litter. So have newspapers: as padding down the back of a rucksack, stuffing inside wet boots, extra insulation below the sleeping bag, wiping pots and pans, to keep under cooking utensils standing on the grass in the interests of hygiene, wearing beneath a sweater if it becomes colder than you expected, mopping up spilled drinks, helping to start fires, for lavatory paper and for reading, for instance.

## First-aid kit

Bandage, lint, adhesive tape, stretch fabric elastoplast, small scissors, safety pins, cotton wool and tube of antiseptic ointment.

## Bivi bag

This 500-gauge polythene survival bag envelopes you if cut off by night or blizzard. Simply climb inside and wait until conditions improve—with your body heat trapped around you.

## Ice axe

Vital on any winter hill walk. Use it to brake if you slip, but practise on your local snowdrift first as described in either *Survival for Young People* or *Climbing for Young People*. Carry the axe strapped to your pack on the way to the hills; then carry it in one hand as you begin to gain height. Expert guidance is needed from an older and responsible person who knows the ropes for this kind of excursion. And you will also need previous experience of summer walks and camps.

# HOW TO TAKE TENTAGE ON A BICYCLE TOUR

Tentage is another word for camping impedimenta. But the first thing is to check that your cycle is oiled, cleaned, aligned, adjusted and running so well it will freewheel miles uphill and the pedals spin in the wind when you lift your shoes off them. And yet the machine will brake on a 10p-piece (or a dime or nickel come to that), with the tyre treads being so good that they will bury that raised rim of coin when the edge of the metal is pressed in between them.

Cycle touring is a great way to see superb countryside and rather safer than backpacking as you are, after all, usually traversing tarred surfaces, and nearer civilisation because of that.

But you cannot always count on things going smoothly. In bad weather a bicycle ride can turn into a living hell as, lashed by rain and wind, you battle your way onwards with no earthly chance of pitching camp until, perhaps, a mile or two more before you can reach a safe and sheltered place to recover.

## Clothing

The same principles as for backpacking apply here: wear thin layers to trap the air between (and carry spare clothing too). You might favour a track suit, for example, only do have tee-shirt, thin jerseys and long john underpants underneath when the weather forecast promises cool temperatures. Long wool socks are also invaluable and can be worn with track suit or whenever you wear cut-down blue jean shorts. Raincape, hat and leggings are wet weather extras—plenty of choice here, too. Either a sou-wester or nylon yachting-type peaked cap will do for the head, while many cyclists prefer wet bare legs to any kind of covering in the rain (and you always have those long warm socks, anyway). Anoraks are sometimes preferred to capes.

### Shoes

Training shoes or cycling shoes (low cut with a thin sole and low heels) are suitable, whichever you are most likely to own.

### Cycle bags

The illustration shows the variety available: you do not have to buy them all at once, however. The first rule is: avoid stowing everything over the back wheel. A large saddlebag and two

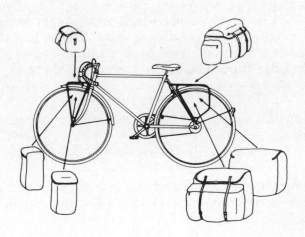

*Karrimor Cycle Bags and Carrier*

smaller front panniers on each side of the front wheel will be fine at first, and probably in the long run. Those wanting to pack extras might later choose to take a handlebar bag, but this is really loading you down. Alternatively, you might sell your saddlebag and sport two rear panniers instead. There is plenty of choice. Just saddle and handlebar bags could do, too.

What to pack inside and how to pack it is described in Chapter 6. It is enough to say just now that you should never carry a rucksack on a bicycle, and that your cycle bags need to be balanced or your steed will wobble. Keep the weight low. Secure the panniers at their base as well as at the top otherwise they will swing out on country road corners. To this end you also need . . .

### Cycle bag carriers

You need really rigid pannier carriers on front or back wheels—depending where the panniers are. They must not sway as you move the pedals or under the weight of the bags. Buy them only from a good cycle shop to make sure this will not happen. Also check the carriers will keep saddlebag or handlebar bag from pressing on the mud guard too.

### Maps

The Ordnance Survey 1:50,000 maps are quite satisfactory for cycle tours.

### Tools

A puncture repair outfit and dumb-bell spanner are basic essentials for the young cyclist trying a first-time camping trip.

## CANOE TOURING WITH TENT AND TRACKSUIT

The canoe is the most realistic boat for young people. It is cheaper than a yacht or powerboat, and feels a lot more sporting. Virtually the one half of a catamaran (without a sail), its speed in a lively current will give any young intrepid the impression of piloting a Cat in a big sea wind. It is indeed ideal for taking a tent on tour through river foam, under the trees, across lens-like pools and wherever the spray flies off rocks.

Canoe touring is an excellent canoe club activity. However, there is nothing to stop you actually making mini canoe camping tours along streams, rivers, canals or lakes even if there is no canoe club immediately at hand or you are too young to join anyway, so long as . . . *you have an older, responsible and experienced person to go with you. And preferably also a friend or two in their own canoes who are equally keen. And that you yourself comply with all the following basic safety rules.*

EVEN BEFORE YOU EVER THINK OF COLLECTING THE EQUIPMENT FOR A SHORT CAMPING TRIP BY CANOE YOU MUST BE ABLE TO SWIM AT LEAST 50 YARDS LIGHTLY CLOTHED. YOU WILL ALWAYS WEAR A LIFEJACKET OR BUOYANCY AID (JUST WHICH WE WILL SEE LATER). ·

YOUR CANOE WILL CONTAIN IN-BUILT BUOYANCY IN THE FORM OF POLYSTYRENE BLOCKS WHICH WILL STILL LET YOUR CRAFT FLOAT AFTER IT HAS CAPSIZED. YOU WILL NEVER WEAR WELLINGTONS, HEAVY CLOTHING, A RUCKSACK OR ANYTHING ELSE SO RIDICULOUS (AS HAS HAPPENED OCCASIONALLY).

YOU LEARN TO CAPSIZE AND LEAVE YOUR CANOE IN SAFE, SHALLOW POOLS FIRST. YOU AVOID MAKING SUCH A TRIP ALONE AND FORGET ABOUT EVER VENTURING ON A FAST RIVER, ESTUARY OR THE SEA UNTIL YOU HAVE GAINED LOTS OF EXPERIENCE FIRST AND JOINED A CANOE CLUB.

THE NEXT SAFETY RULES CONCERN THE WATER ITSELF. CHECK THAT IT IS SAFE. YOU MAY KNOW IT FROM LOCAL KNOWLEDGE, FOR INSTANCE, OR YOU CAN ASK THE BRITISH CANOE UNION SENDING A STAMPED ADDRESSED ENVELOPE. THE BCU ALSO PUBLISH *A GUIDE TO WATERWAYS* WHICH DETAILS RIVERS, AND GRADES THEIR DIFFICULTY: YOUR LOCAL LIBRARY SHOULD HAVE A COPY.

Finally, access . . . Rivers like the Wye and Severn have ancient rights of navigation so that it is possible to canoe long stretches legally. The majority of fishing rivers in Britain, however, have severely restricted access: even, for instance, in the upper stretches of the Wye. The local British Canoe Union Adviser (name obtainable from BCU) will advise you about landowners and angling societies to approach for permission. In the case of the larger navigable rivers, apply to the local river board for a permit, and to the Inland Waterways Board in the case of canals.

## Canoes and paddles

The kind of canoe a young person is likely to have already is either a general touring canoe made from glassfibre, or a slalom canoe of the same material. While the modern slalom canoe is the wrong shape for carrying camping gear—it is far too slender—the older kind of slalom canoe will accommodate the gear and can be adapted for a river trip so long as the young paddler has already proved he or she can master what is a notoriously unstable craft in the hands of the beginner. You have to be able to balance the craft, and recover your balance immediately any time it starts to go over with a range of paddle strokes that are really technical. They call for a lot of practice first on safe familiar water. Your paddles should be of a size to go with the canoeist. Choose them by reaching a hand upwards as you stand against a paddle and curl your fingers over the edge of the top blade—that's about the length you want. Slalom paddles are available from any canoe shop, and you can buy general-purpose canoe paddles in kit form.

Although the diagram shows a spare pair of split paddles attached to the rear decks of the canoe with shock cord elastic this precaution is probably not needed for what should be a very non-serious river trip. However, keep in mind the need for spare paddle just in case you ever lose the ones in your fists on anything approaching a longer canoe tour. They're a must.

So is a spraysheet over the cockpit to keep everything dry inside. So is your map inside a plastic cover strapped to the deck in front of you by two strips of shock cord elastic knotted through four holes in the deck (as shown). And so are two toggles at stern and bows instead just of nylon loops; again as illustrated.

The reason is that if you capsize and grasp a small nylon loop at either end, and then the canoe twists over and over in the current, you will lose your fingers trapped in such loops. A toggle, however, allows the canoe to spin and the toggle remains in the same position in your grip.

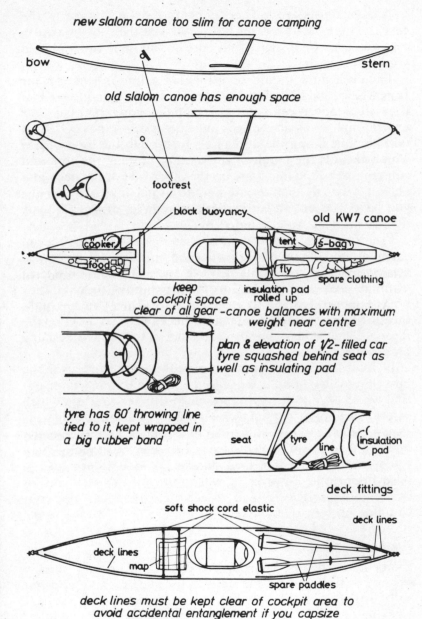

new slalom canoe too slim for canoe camping

bow                                                    stern

old slalom canoe has enough space

footrest

block buoyancy                        old KW7 canoe

cooker                                    tent   s-bag

food                                       fly

keep                                        spare clothing
cockpit space                    insulation pad
clear of all gear - canoe balances with maximum
                weight near centre

plan & elevation of 1/2-filled car
tyre squashed behind seat as
well as insulating pad

tyre has 60' throwing line
tied to it, kept wrapped in
a big rubber band          seat    tyre  line  insulation
                                              pad

deck fittings

soft shock cord elastic

deck lines

deck lines

map

spare paddles

deck lines must be kept clear of cockpit area to
avoid accidental entanglement if you capsize

Canoe Touring Equipment

The last 'musts' are two decklines for the front and rear of the canoe. These, however, must not run past the cockpit area in case you capsize or they could possibly entangle you and hold you under the water.

The deck lines should be grippable nylon or a man-made rope which floats. Their position is shown in the diagram. How they are attached can vary. For example, you might pass one end through a hole in the deck and knot it below the deck. Now take the line along the deck, pass it through the loop of line which anchors the toggle at the stern or bows of the craft and run the rest of the line back up the other side of the deck and anchor it with a quick release knot to a small loop of nylon line you have 'glassed' on to the deck. Any holes drilled for deck fittings must be waterproofed by 'glassing'.

Your deck line now serves two purposes. If you capsize, you can grab the canoe and deckline on surfacing; it gives you something to hold on to. If, however, you stop above a stretch of rapids, and examine these from the riverbank to find if they are too serious for you to shoot them . . . Then you can undo the quick release knot of one of the deck lines and, holding the free end, 'line' your canoe down the side of the rapids like a dog on a lead.

If you still have to buy a canoe, however, avoid any rush. The best thing you can do is write to the British Canoe Union and find which is your nearest canoe club affiliated to it and which offers training in basic techniques. This is invaluable, as experts teach you to paddle their own canoes, and when ready you can take the BCU Proficiency Test which will require you to conform to an established standard of safe watermanship. Also important, however: it will show you the best kind of canoe most suited to *you*. Meanwhile, you can do your camping on foot or by bike.

## Clothing

Canoeing is the one sport where you warm up very quickly sitting down. Paddle five minutes in the rain on a lake, and you will probably still feel warm in just a tee-shirt, your legs working on the footrests as well as your arms on the paddles. It is the wind that cools the canoeist down. So several thin layers of clothing are again the ideal—they can be shed or added when necessary: vest, shirt, sweater, anorak, shorts and training shoes are all OK. And the track suit? It's great for changing into at your camp site especially if it is still dry. In winter, or when you may be in the water for some time, wet suit trousers—like Long Johns—are safest. You can buy them in kit form.

**Lifejackets and buoyancy aids**

Most schools, colleges, youth organisations and outdoor centres supply lifejackets for beginners—as opposed to the buoyancy aid which is really a sort of waistcoat padded with plastic foam. The reason is that a lifejacket when inflated will support an unconscious body face up. However, on inland water people rarely use a lifejacket in a fully inflated state, so in these conditions there is really nothing to choose between them. You should know, however, that the controversy exists. Many experienced paddlers prefer the buoyancy aid because it is more comfortable, does not restrict their paddle strokes and provides good insulation. It is also easier to swim in a buoyancy aid than in a lifejacket. It is just that in a real crisis the inflated lifejacket is the only thing which will hold an unconscious person face upwards (providing, of course, the casualty has the presence of mind to inflate his lifejacket when the emergency happens). In sea-canoeing it is essential to wear a lifejacket. Whether lifejacket or buoyancy aid is used, it is important that it is the correct size for the paddler and is fastened correctly and bears the BSI kite mark.

**Canoe bags**

First of all know the dangers of packing your canoe with the packages needed for camping. They must be securely attached so that if you capsize they cannot jam you in the cockpit or float out. This could happen if you ram a rock or river bank head-on. The sudden jolt could slide an unattached cargo in the space behind the cockpit forward so it slams you in the back. If the canoe capsizes you could now be wedged inside by the objects which have moved forward, and you might be unable to get out quickly enough. So tie each bag to a loop of nylon line 'glassed' into the shell of your boat at the appropriate point.

Quite a lot of space inside the canoe will be taken up with the block buoyancy in bows and stern as shown in the diagram. Don't try removing this or you could weaken your canoe. Instead, pack your gear into small packages which will fit against the slabs of plastic foam that keep the canoe floating even though it might have capsized. Your tent, for instance, should be split into two or three packages; flysheet, poles and inner tent. This will have more chance of fitting inside neatly than the tent in one parcel. Work out the size of each bag you need first. And don't plan to have each bag stuffed full. Half-filled bags are easier to pack.

Make waterproof bags from 500-gauge polythene tubing. Anything thinner will tear. The bottom edges of the tube can be sealed by placing them between a piece of kitchen foil folded over, and ironing over the foil. To strengthen this seam fold the plastic over two or three times and clip it in place with the large fasteners you can buy at stationers.

To secure the top, grip the packed bag together at the top, spin it round and throttle the neck with a piece of plastic-covered three-core electrical wire in a reef knot. Then fold over the end of the bag back down past the neck and hold in place with a thick rubber band—the kind you might cut from an old car inner tube.

Test your bags are waterproof first by dunking them in a bathful of water—when packed.

Another form of useful container for smaller objects is the plastic sweet jar used by sweetshops, newsagents, tobacconists and so on. Ask around the shops you know for the empty ones (often they are thrown away): they will prove invaluable.

## Throwing line and inner tube

It is important to pack 60 feet of lightweight line just to the rear of your canoe seat so that in an emergency you could throw it to someone else in trouble on the water. Nylon is one material, but a better one might be one of the synthetic ropes which float. One end of it should be tied in a knot to make it all the easier to hold in your hand, and the other end is tied round an old car inner tube which just fits—half inflated—in the space behind your seat. The diagram shows the position, and there are two good reasons why it is best here. One: it serves as a buffer between your packages stowed at the rear of the canoe, should they ever break from their anchoring loops, and you: and two: it can serve as a comfortable support for the lower part of your back as you paddle. In an emergency though it will act as a giant quoit which—with practice first—you can throw with ease and so send out your lightweight line from the bank to help others.

If you are carrying an insulating foam pad this too can be stashed behind the seat (rolled up with a strong rubber band)—sometimes, however, there is no room for this and the tyre. In which case the tyre should have priority as it is a survival aid. (And you can always use it as a pillow in camp too).

## First-aid kit
The same as for backpacking.

## Canoe repair kit
This should contain: a *small hacksaw blade* for cutting out bashed-in glassfibre; *rag* for wiping glassfibre dry; *meths and matches* so you can rub on meths and set it on fire to evaporate any water around the hole; *waterproof adhesive canoe tape* (it won't work unless the surface of canoe is dry): *Sylglas tape* for patching holes (obtainable from hardware stores—cut just so much off before you begin your trip): *Araldite Rapid Adhesive* comes in two tubes and fills a hole so giving body for the adhesive tape to go on over the top; *a spare footrest bolt*; *needle and thread* for repairing ripped spraysheets.

## Bivi bag
The same as for bagpacking, just in case you have to spend a night out without your tent.

## Food and vacuum flask
Chew energy-boosting food as you canoe (carried in your pockets), but also take a flask of hot coffee or tea. That's a great help when you may be flagging.

## Maps and guidebooks

The Ordnance Survey 1:50,000 sheets are fine (wrapped in plastic to keep dry), but a larger scale map is even better as it shows more of the river details. And the BCU *Guide to Waterways* is necessary too where your river is listed.

## Canoe trolly

A car roofrack is the best way to carry your canoe, but you can also tow it behind your bicycle or, even as you walk, on a canoe trolley. Make one of these from an old pair of pram wheels and some wood.

## Sponge

A big car-cleaning sponge will mop up water in the canoe and also wipe down your tent, especially the underside of the groundsheet.

## Spraysheet ripcord

It is vital you can tear away the spraysheet from the cockpit rim if you capsize. Either stitch a toggle securely to the front of the spraysheet OR a cord across the spraysheet sewing each end of this line back underneath the elastic edges of the spraysheet (so, when pulled, it really does curl the elastic up and rips the spraysheet right off).

# 5   How to Pitch a Tent

Putting up the tent you have just bought or borrowed is really easy—if you have practised first on a flat piece of ground. Without such tentative runs, however, there are few things more awkward, especially in rain, wind and with darkness approaching. Poles, seams, zips, toggles, loops, cords, flaps, tapes, pegs and guylines then become a Chinese puzzle with time limits fast running out.

At the Outward Bound school where I instructed, students faced a number of initiative tests during each course. The one they found by far the toughest was not the swinging across a chasm on a rope carrying a bucket of nitro-glycerine for blowing out an oil well gusher on the other side, nor balancing across an alligator-infested pool on a greasy log while helping a wounded companion on a rope stretcher . . . it was putting up a small tent blindfold!

The problem is that pitching a tent requires close attention to detail. And if you have just been involved in physical exertion—backpacking or canoeing, say—the sudden switch can catch you by surprise. It's rather like that riddle, in fact, where a deaf and dumb man goes into a store to buy a hammer.

'How does he ask for it?' you say to friends, the answer being to move a fist up and down as if pounding on the counter.

'Then,' you say, 'a blind man followed him. He wanted a pair of scissors.

'How did he ask for those?'

Almost certainly someone will move their hands as if snipping through a piece of paper.

'No,' you say. 'He just asked for them.'

It is this kind of response, however, that you put into tent pitching when biceps, abdominals, deltoids, pectorals, lattisimus dorsi and all the other big muscles in your body have been straining to the limit, and then suddenly you are asking only your fingers and thumbs to do all the work. Not to mention that part of the brain which deals with geometry, as the angles of your tent have all to be adjusted for strength and comfort. There will be times consequently when, as a result, you suddenly feel too tired to think straight. You cannot be bothered.

And your camp suffers, hastily planned and roughly rigged—a possibly dangerous situation if the weather turns bad in the night. It will certainly be uncomfortable. Yet how different pitching your tent becomes when you have practised it beforehand so thoroughly you can do it in your sleep— virtually blindfold, in fact.

## TWO TRICKS TO BEAT YOUR SYSTEM

Your own nervous system, that is. The one which, possibly over-stretched and at the end of a day backpacking to your camp site, will have you trying still to put your best foot forward when you should now be putting your best hand forward instead.

Here are two very basic hints which will always help you find that energy to pitch camp. Practise using them during your first sessions with that new tent even if it is only on the lawn.

### Tent pole survival kit: Mark I

Look at your tent poles and check their length and diameter. Why? Because you are now about to fit inside them one or two tubes which contain food supplies should you ever need them in emergency—rations like broken-up Kendal mint or salted peanuts (but not chocolate, which melts). Clear plastic $\frac{3}{8}$in hose bought from a hardware store is an example of a tube which will fit inside many tent poles. It can be sealed at both ends with corks bought from a chemists shop and cut down to size with a sharp Stanley knife, and will keep the contents dry and safe inside the tube. And it is in fact a revival kit (more than survival) to boost fading energy on arrival at a camp site. Chew the rations as soon as you begin to put up the tent; you will be surprised at the difference such a snack can make.

And how does this emergency food supply stay locked inside the tent poles yet appear when needed? Let's look at the second survival kit you can also store inside your tent poles first, then go into how to hide them away until wanted.

## Tent pole survival kit: Mark II

Four or five small tubes are needed here. One containing matches; another, solid Meta fuel broken small for heating water; a third, containing coffee or tea; a fourth, powdered milk; and a fifth, if you take it, sugar. Needless to say, they should all be sealed tightly.

The matches tube should double-seal the matches by the following safety method: break the matches in half first, then pack them into two or three plastic drinking straws head to tail so their heads never touch; the ends of the straws are then sealed in a match flame and the straws are slipped into the plastic hose which is corked tight.

The tube containing the Meta solid fuel should have a striking colour or marking so you never mistake it for food.

How you use this fuel to brew up tea or coffee when you have lost everything—except, I hope, a cooking pot or tin can in which to heat the water—is simple. Arrange two or three small stones on the ground to make a pot stand and place the solid fuel between these on a thin flat piece of stone or slate. Light with a match and heat a little water in the pan (with lid) to which you add more as it gets hot. You need some draught, but not so much it dissipates the heat by scattering the flames. Adjust the stones—perhaps adding more—until the heat is at its maximum, something which you need to practise during those early camping sessions.

MAKE USE OF THESE REVIVAL KITS DURING YOUR FIRST PRACTICE SESSIONS BY ALL MEANS. ON PROPER CAMPING TRIPS, HOWEVER, KEEP SUCH AIDS PACKED AWAY READY INSIDE THE TENT POLES AS SURVIVAL KITS IN CASE YOU EVER NEED AN EMERGENCY SOURCE OF HEAT AND SUSTENANCE. NORMALLY YOU WILL USE THE TEA BAGS, MILK AND SUGAR STASHED IN YOUR RUCKSACK, CYCLE BAG OR WHATEVER, AND THE FOOD STOWED IN YOUR POCKETS FOR CHEWING DURING THE DAY BEFORE YOU EVER REACH THAT EVENING CAMP SITE.

## How the survival kits are packed inside the tent poles

A good tent will have its tent poles linked by thick shockcord elastic which is threaded inside the individual sections of each pole. It makes the fitting together of the tent poles much easier as everything is already linked together even when packed away. If this is the case with your tent you simply push your survival kits inside sections of tent pole and they will stay put so long as you checked the diameters of your tent poles and plastic tubes first. The elastic locks the tubes in place.

A couple of hints. The thickness of shockcord elastic is such that the ⅜in plastic tube described may prove too bulky to fit inside the tent poles as well in which case you need to buy the next thickness of plastic hose down; say around ¼in diameter tubing. It does not hold as much but the supplies contained will still be adequate in an emergency if you pack away as many tubes as possible.

The actual packing will be usually confined to the two middle sections of each tent pole. What happens is you may well have four sections to one tent pole. Each section will have one wide-open mouth and one narrow end (where it slides into the next section's wide end). You will find that the only accessible ends for your survival kits are the two wide-open mouths of the middle sections as shown in the diagram. You push your survival tubes down inside these two middle sections until the far end narrows and stops you pushing any more. You must leave two or three inches clear at the wide-open end too (so the next narrow-ended section can slip into it unimpeded).

How, you will ask, are you going to free those plastic tubes jammed away inside the metal poles when you may desperately need them? Its easy.

Imagine you have your tubes ready to push inside a section of the tent pole one after the other. The first tube you push inside should *push ahead of it a paper clip squashed into a ball with a pair of pliers*. To this 'ball' is tied a length of thin but strong twine. Now as you push the rest of the tubes down inside the section of tent pole the twine lies alongside them and hangs from the wide-open mouth of the metal pole ready for you to pull like a ripcord. Pull! and the metal 'ball' will drag the plastic tubes out one after the other as you tug.

To get the contents out from their plastic tubes in a hurry is

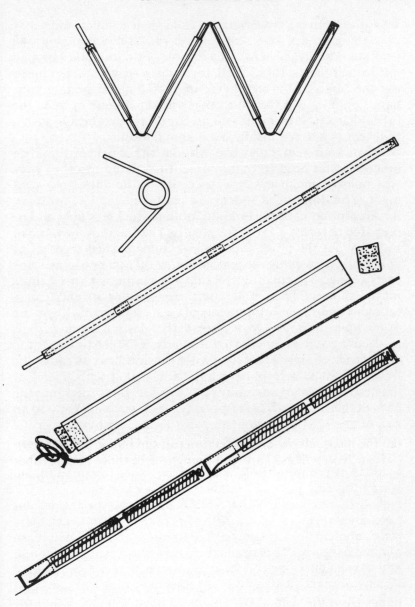

*Tent Pole Survival Kits*

easy if the tubes are well-sealed, and their contents kept dry; everything pours out salt-cellar-style. But supposing the peanuts, Meta fuel or whatever have got damp and jammed inside their plastic tube? Well, for a start you will still be able to use the Meta fuel even when damp. And as for getting your hands on it . . . slit the tube open with a penknife or bend the tubes sharply bit by bit as you do a toothpaste tube. Or push a thin tent peg down inside. That should do it.

When your tent poles are without the shockcord linkage described you need to make some: then fixing together your tent poles is much easier—especially in the dark on a wild night. You don't need shockcord elastic either. Use ordinary flat elastic—as used for holding football stockings up—and be prepared to renew it fairly frequently. The diagram shows how. First lay out the poles with their sections pushed together as you would in pitching the tent. Measure off a piece of elastic for each connected tent pole so that the elastic is two or three inches shorter. Then pull apart the sections of each pole, though keeping the components of each pole separate from the other pole or poles. Now thread the elastics through their respective sections, anchoring the ends of the elastic inside the end of each complete tent pole with the wire clips you can make from big thick wire paper clips (bent round with pliers) as illustrated. How you actually locate these wire springs into the ends of their respective tent poles is a trick—having knotted an end of the elastic through one of the wire springs, push the spring right up inside the tent pole with a knitting needle or thin stick until it reaches the end—as shown. The individual sections of each tent pole will then be under tension and will spring together as you straighten each section out.

And therein lies a WARNING! Fitting elastic inside tent poles gives them a Jack-in-a-Box life of their own. Leave them for a moment folded up, yet free to move and they will jump about like squibs. This spoils the ends of each tent pole section and causes 'burrs' or roughnesses on the metal edges. Result? When you next fit two ends together they jam and you can't pull them apart. The answer is always to handle your tent poles most carefully and avoid, even when fitting two sections together, knocking metal against metal.

If they do jam together, hold the join for two or three seconds (that's all, no longer!) in a match flame. This will expand the outer tent pole edge long enough for you to be able to twist the inner pole free. Then clean up the edges of the two sections with the rough side of the matchbox to smooth out the roughnesses so they no longer stick together.

## HOW TO CHOOSE A CRICKET PITCH CAMP SITE

What have pitching a tent and pitching a cricket ball in common? The answer is: the need to direct either item on to the one piece of ground most suited to it that is just out of range of being clobbered (in the tent's case, by the wind). Why not, you might say, pitch it a long way from being clobbered? Well, we all know what happens to long hops, full tosses and wides. And pitching a tent too far from the breeze on a stiflingly hot day in mid-summer will stifle you just too much. You need to strike a balance as conditions are always changing.

So how do you select your practice 'pitch' (for this is also the name for the patch on which your tent will stand as well as a place for delivering cricket balls)? Begin now by looking for an appropriate grassy plot in your backyard, on the lawn, in a field or even in your local park—so long as nobody objects (you do NOT intend sleeping there in this case).

It helps to look from the cricket groundsman's point of view. He lives for his stretch of turf, even to rolling a tent on wheels over it when rain threatens to spoil the wicket. Yes, the covers. The following tips are the kind of things he does himself to check the ground is as perfect as conditions allow for the day's play . . .

PEERING: check the ground is as level as possible at the point where you intend pitching the tent (just as the groundsman concentrates on the twenty two yard stretch of wicket on which the actual play takes place). Your pitch need only be dead flat for the amount of turf your tent covers which, in the case of a one-man tent, is little more than the room taken up by your body lying on the ground. And for a two-man tent, not all that much more. Either way, it means the surrounding ground may slope unevenly, but so long as you spot a flatiron of grass big enough just to accommodate you that will be just the job.

FEELING: first, you need to feel the actual ground under your shoes; second, the softest breeze even chilling your wetted fingers. Test the spring in the ground. Does it 'feel' good? Simply by standing on it? Or does your bouncing step produce moisture bubbling up from the earth? You want something firm, flat and dry. The wind direction—even if it is only a zephyr right now—is important; it must not blow into your tent door. Knowing its direction means you can pitch the tent's tail into it. And therefore your pitch, if only just big enough to house the tent, should point in that general direction. If your pitch, however, is on the small side, but points across the wind, then this could be the way you pitch your tent as an alternative—at right angles to the breeze.

KNEELING: next check how much wind there is. The tent should be sheltered from it, but many people forget that their tent will stand only waist high or under. This is all the protection required to take the brunt of the wind from hitting your shelter. Although a strong wind is slamming your face, therefore, it may be relatively becalmed a foot or two lower down. So kneel down to test it, especially when there is no obvious shelter. A fold in the ground might just be adequate when your low-level checking shows little disturbance at tent height.

PRODDING: stick a tent peg or penknife through the turf to check the soil is free from stones, rocks or water an inch or two down.

CUTTING: cut away or pull up any large hanks of grass that otherwise make a potentially flat grass plot lumpy.

SWEEPING: clear away stones, pebbles, sheep muck etc. with the edge of a hand.

ROLLING: lie on the pitch and test it for 'feel' again. Roll over on it, and remove any hard spots—say large stones buried just beneath the surface. The pitch may now be found to slope rather more than it did on first appearance.

All this may not seem important when pitching your tent now. Still carry out the system, however. It helps you learn the right habits early. Eventually you carry them out without thinking; an automatic reaction.

## WHAT HAPPENS WHEN THE INSTRUCTIONS ARE MISSING

Obviously you follow the instructions accompanying a new or borrowed tent. What happens however when they are missing? Forget about it and go camping without first trying to pitch your tent, and you will be left in the dark when the time does come to pitch camp.

Besides helping you work out a system for that particular tent in your own time and safe surroundings, tent-pitching exercises at home give you other opportunities too. Checking there are no rips or pinpricks in the tent panels, for instance. And that no poles are missing, all the pegs are there and the doors actually do fasten.

This way you can complain in good time over faults, and get them put right. Or, if you borrowed the tent, at least you have drawn attention to the damage before you actually use the shelter.

### The trick that says it all about tent pitching

Take three coins and stress you are about to do something simple so slowly in front of your friends that they should have no difficulty at all in following your movements. And that although you will only do it once, the same thing stands: your movements will be dead simple. Yet you can bet someone will get that sequence wrong.

Place the three coins on a table, then pick them up saying 'One, two three'. Now put them back on the table again— 'Four, five, six'. Pick up two of them saying 'Seven, eight'. Then place these back down again saying 'Nine, ten'.

Now hand someone the coins and ask him to do exactly what you did. Very often they will put down the coins saying 'One, two, three . . .' And their counting goes haywire. The reason being they had not been watching you quite as closely as they thought.

It is a good illustration of what happens when you first pitch a tent. You open the bag and unfold the tent, remembering, you are sure, the way it is folded, where the poles are stowed and how the pegs are stored away. Yet come the time when you have to take the tent down and pack it up, many of these simple details have quite deserted you. It's important, too. Stuff your shelter away carelessly, and you may not even be able to squash it into its bag—let alone the pegs and poles as well. And any desperate forcing will harm the tent.

So make a conscious effort to remember how everything came out of the bag—which seam-went-where-and-what-pole-was-pushed-into-the-other-pole kind of thing, even if you have to pencil details on the back of an envelope to do it.

Remember to ask someone to help you. Tent-pitching is much easier in pairs, although a system is described later for those who are on their own. And do keep rainproofs handy even when practising. It is a point to watch wherever you are.

## Two-pole tent without a groundsheet

This simple tent will probably be made from cotton, could be home-made and there might be one stored away in the coal house or attic. Basic as such shelters are, they need patience in pitching.

Spread the tent flat on the ground and fasten up the door—probably in this case by tying tapes with bows, or with a zip or press studs.

The two poles are now inserted into the tent, rear pole first. Push the spindle end of this up through the appropriate grommet hole in the ridge seam, and have the pole held upright. Now take the two guylines attached to the tent by this hole and—after pulling them out one after the other—attach them each to a tent peg (as described a little later in this chapter) placed firmly in the ground.

Repeat this procedure with the front pole. However, someone should still stand guard over the first pole you erected (the rear one) as if you let go too soon at this stage the shelter will collapse and you will have to start again.

Before you peg out the shorter guys attached first to the corners then sides of the tent, re-align the front and rear pair of guylines so the tent, even in only a semi-pitched state, still stands reasonably square.

Check the bottom edges where tent meets grass for metal eyelets or small loops which must be skewered to the ground. Go from one such anchor point to the next, keeping the material between well adjusted, but not—remember, this is cotton which shrinks when damp—drum tight. Finally adjust all the guylines so the ridge is straight and the shelter has no unnecessary folds. The roof and walls will thus be fully extended, all the angles symmetrical.

There may be a border of absorbent cloth along the base of the tent walls (called a sod cloth or mudwall) for preventing draughts and mopping up the damp. You can either squash this to the ground with heavy stones on top or, more usually, tuck it inside so the groundsheet edges rest on top.

Strong 500-gauge polythene is best here—as you used for the timberline tent. Lay it out by pulling it sideways and diagonally as you peg the corners to stretch it as smoothly as possible between these anchor points. Meat skewers will do for pegs. Push them through the double thickness of groundsheet corners tucked back for extra strength.

Lastly, place stub plates—tin lids, for example—beneath the tent poles; fasten the door once more and square up the tent for the last time by readjusting guys and if necessary, pegs.

## Two-pole tent with separate groundsheet

This tent is the same as the one just described above, but has its own groundsheet. Small metal rings stitched to the base of the tent walls correspond with identical rings around the rim of the groundsheet. Start by fastening the door.

Simply smooth out the groundsheet on the grass, place the collapsed tent on top of it—door away from the wind—and push pegs (or meat skewers) through the metal rings on the tent and then through the other rings on the ground sheet which tally with them. Incidentally, try to ensure the tent walls are just outside the groundsheet perimeter as you do this, rather than have the groundsheet edges showing.

Put the tent poles inside the tent and place them, spindle first through the grommet holes, then blunt end on the stub plates. Then peg out the main guys at each end which hold the tent poles upright. Close the door, peg out the corner guys. Then the side guys. Lastly, square everything up.

### Two-pole tent with fitted groundsheet

A wall to wall groundsheet already attached to the actual tent was the one refinement of the hang glider tent described in Chapter 2. It makes tent pitching that much easier. You pin the groundsheet to the ground first—tent material loose on top—then raise the roof exactly as just detailed above.

### Two-pole tent with fitted groundsheet and flysheet attached on top

Originally flysheets were an afterthought. First, the tent was pitched, then the flysheet was added on top as extra protection. Many tents still exist which use this principle: you have to pitch the tent before erecting the flysheet.

Drape the fly over the tent, push the tent pole spindles through the flysheet grommet holes (which should fit just as they did for the tent), then peg out the fly evenly to the ground.

Check that the flysheet does not touch the tent at any point. You saw why in Chapter 2.

### Two-pole flysheet* where tent with fitted groundsheet is suspended inside

Here is the modern idea where—you saw it with the timberline tent—the flysheet is pitched first in bad weather (and indeed can be used as a shelter in its own right during fine conditions). The tent itself is then hung inside this, its groundsheet finally pegged to the ground.

It is a very convenient method, and many modern tents use it—some with a ridgepole stretching beneath the ridge of the fly for extra stability, and other refinements like wrap-around bell ends which give the flysheet an absolutely all-round protective cover.

Pitch the flysheet as you pitched the two-pole tent without a groundsheet—the first tent type described above. The poles are inserted through the grommet holes, the guylines pegged out

*Yes, it's still called a 'tent'.

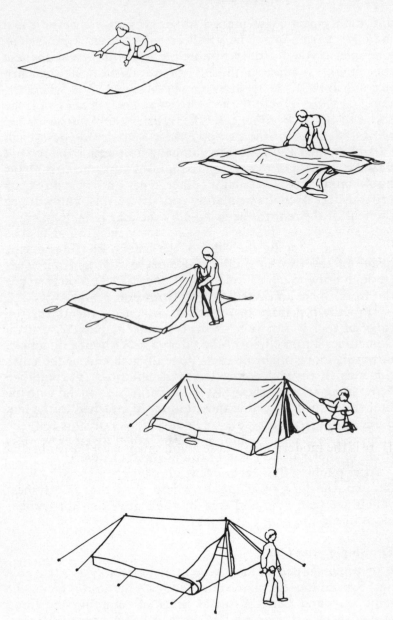

*Cotton Tent with Separate Groundsheet*

and the flysheet edges pinned to the ground. However, there may be variations. The flysheet might use A-poles, for example, as you did for the timberline tent—though in this case they might straddle both ends of the flysheet (though not necessarily). Or, the flysheet may be of the 'A' type where the tent poles are slid into sleeves at front and rear, and assume the shape of an 'A'. In either case, the flysheet is still pitched to the same system as for the two-pole ridge tent already described.

And the tent itself? Before you hang it up inside the fly, put down your strip of closed cell foam insulating pad first. Then hook up the tent (actually, inner tent) and peg down its groundsheet over the insulating pad. To do this, you will peg the rear of the tent to the ground by the rear pole, then crawl back towards the entrance, pegging down the groundsheet as you go and clipping the sides of the tent to the rings on the inside of the fly—so pulling the sides of the tent outwards (though not enough to touch the flysheet itself). You then peg the front of the inner tent by the front pole.

How the top ridge of the tent is attached beneath the top ridge of the fly can vary; it depends on the maker's system. Sometimes hooks clip over the ridgepole. Without a ridgepole, however, loops might be used—one at each end of the tent's ridge which are each connected to the tent poles (the tent then being slung between these fastenings rather as you did with the timberline shelter). (How these loops are attached to the tent poles also differs; the poles may have hooks or slots for each loop, and each separate loop might be joined together by press studs so they can be passed around the tent pole.)

After pitching flysheet and tent, check there is space between the two—nothing touching anywhere. And that the flysheet panels are held firm and taut by their guys or short rubber loops along the base of the fabric.

## The single pole tent

A pyramid-shaped tent is put up in the same way as a two pole one. Spread the tent on the ground, check the door is facing the right way and peg the metal rings surrounding the fitted groundsheet to the ground; starting at one corner of the tent, moving on to the next and so on—checking the groundsheet is fully pulled out and not wrinkled. Slip the tent pole inside,

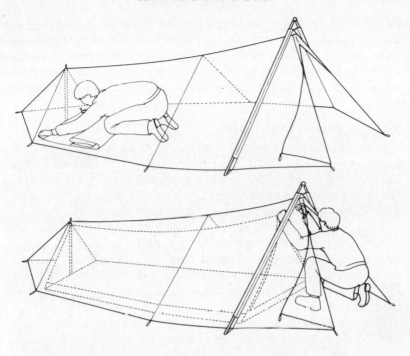

*Inner Tent Pitching X-ray*

push the spindle end of this through the grommet hole, settle the pole upright now on its stub plate and peg out the front guyline. This will hold everything in place as you now peg around the wall guys until everything is well adjusted, tent pole vertical.

## TENT PITCHING TRICKS

Ever since the days of Florence Nightingale and Napoleon— when ridge tents and bell tents were basic accommodation in their individual campaigns—certain principles have held firm for pitching such shelters: the ridge tent, especially, being the mainstay of lightweight tent design today.

They can work like magic too—like, in fact, the illusion where a strongman beats a six-inch nail through a plank of wood with his bare fist. (The head of the nail is actually palmed in a balled-up hanky or duster in his hand, so protecting it during the moment of impact.) This is not all that far removed from camping either, as the best way to plant tent pegs is not by mallet or hammer, but by palming a flat piece of stone, metal or wood and smacking the anchors into the ground as if open-handed.

**Put tent pegs in their place**

The easiest way to knock tent pegs in at the right angle is to turn your back on the tent (like shoeing a horse). This will then ensure the pegs enter the ground at an angle of 45 degrees and that the guylines reach the pegs at an angle of 90 degrees. The pegs moreover should be knocked in up to the eyelet or notch.

Stick pegs for the main guys (and side guys, too) into the ground before you ever raise the tent. You must judge approximately where you think they will go, and at first you will probably be so way out with your guesses that you will have to re-position most of them. Stick at it, though; you will save time doing it this way in the not-so-long run.

Avoid placing pegs too near the tent. Otherwise the sides sag and the fly can actually flutter against the tent when it is windy. Instead place the pegs almost at the limit of their guylines, then use the sliders on them for that final adjustment which pulls out the wrinkles.

Thin steel pegs are needed to penetrate hard ground; they are useless, however, in soggy conditions. You need long wooden or plastic pegs here. When the ground is too hard for pegs, anchor the tent to heavy rocks with the guys (as you did for the Hang Glider and Timberline shelters).

Pegs pushed into the ground and weighted down with heavy stones are bad—the sawing action of the cords on rock frays them quickly.

Bent and twisted pegs should be straightened across the knee or some other edge and not hammered into shape. This weakens them so they can break when most needed.

Always push a couple of spare tent pegs in the ground to one side of the door so you can find them in the dark if you need to anchor a guyline that has come loose.

**Let wind help you raise the roof**

Have you ever had to put on a jacket or anorak with a gale

singing round your ears? Yet it's easy if you turn to face the wind. This blows the jacket at you so that it is easy to slip an arm down one sleeve and then, turning your body away from the wind so the jacket is plastered to it from behind, you can then shrug on the other sleeve too. Try to do this, however, facing away from the wind in the first instance, and you will find it hopeless. The garment is blown away from you like a flag out of reach.

It's the same with a tent. To pitch it in the wind you need to face it. So, always make the point of taking the tail of the tent (or flysheet if it is the flysheet you are putting up first) to the foot of your pitch (as in 'foot of the bed'). And tack that leading edge down first of all. As the rest of the tent is now blown backwards towards you like a wind sock you can pin it down and jack it up quite easily.

There are complications, however, if the position of your site makes the tent whip round as you try to pitch it across wind (though you should be pitching it in the shelter of something solid like a wall, boulder or dip in the ground). The best remedy here is for one of you to lie on the tent material while the other does the pitching.

(Incidentally, when the weather is settled and forecast good, pitch your tent with the door to the south-east or east, so you get the sun on the door as you cook breakfast from your sleeping bag next morning.)

## Go with the good guys

Windy weather buffeting the tent means you need extra guys to the windward side of the shelter—for stability. Any strong cord will do, run from the appropriate tent pole spindle down to its peg.

Last thing at night: slacken off canvas tents which will shrink from dew, let alone rain. If such a tent and its guylines twang everything is too tight. And the tent consequently becomes pulled out of shape for good. Tighten up the guys next morning if it promises to be dry and the tent material likely to slacken off even more. The only tension needed is just enough to remove the wrinkles.

A nylon tent, however, does need to be pulled really taut—as you saw in Chapter 2.

### Pitching miscellany

Sort out your tent poles which by now you should have rigged with elastic linking if shockcord elastic was not already incorporated.

A-poles need metal base plates if the ground is soft otherwise they give no stability to the shelter. Be careful not to rip tent material on the A-pole spike.

If a zip sticks—especially a metal one—rub a pencil along it (as graphite is a lubricant). Forget about oil, however, as you will spoil the tent fabric.

The underside of the groundsheet gets muddy if there is nothing placed under it. While an insulating pad is best, you could also use your plastic survival bag as an under-layer. Whenever the groundsheet does get muddy—sponge it down afterwards.

### Pitching your tent single-handed

Place the tent on the ground and peg out the groundsheet as if there were two of you. Then position the rear pole upright, and keep the guylines taut as you step backwards and peg them down away from the tent. Go back to the rear pole, set it upright once more if it has fallen down—or is about to—and now pull the ridge taut as you back towards the front of the tent. Maintain the tension as you place the front pole upright, then walk backwards pulling on the front guylines now until you can peg these down too: a tip here is you may find it easier to peg these fairly close together at first, then re-peg them at their usual wider angle later as you re-adjust the whole tent. The shelter will now stand drunkenly between the two poles and main guylines. Go round quickly before it falls down and peg the corners and sides out. Once this is done you can re-adjust everything inside properly.

## HOW TO STRIKE A TENT

'Striking your tent' does not mean coming to blows with it (though you may feel like doing this during those first tries to pitch it solo). It means instead taking it down and packing everything away. And in a most important respect it too has something in common with striking a cricket ball—or basketball, poolball, football or baseball come to that. You need the right timing.

A rainy morning is a drag to begin the day with when it was such a great evening last night. Only now you must pack your gear and be on your way. Hurry to pull down the tent and pack your bags so that you get it over with quickly, and you are likely to damage equipment. Do things in the wrong order, as well you might if you have not practised first, and again your gear suffers.

The first rule is: pack everything else first, and leave your tent until last. This gives you shelter as you stash everything away. By the time the tent comes down all you need do is to slip it on top of the rucksack, cycle bag or whatever and that's it.

Secondly: if you can, wait until it is at least fair before you dismantle the tent. The ideal is to air your tent in sunlight first before rolling it up, the flysheet being draped separately from a branch, on a boulder or over a wall. However, even though it may be obvious the sun is not going to break through, at least a pause from the rain will allow you to shake a lot of moisture off the fly and this helps.

The order in which you do strike your tent is usually the exact opposite of how you pitched the tent. What you did last then, you now undo first. The general system being:

**Clear the tent**
Crumbs, feathers and any rubbish left on the groundsheet should be removed. Sponge down anything spilt.

**Remove the pegs**
Pull out those pegs anchoring the sides and corners of the tent, but leave those securing the main guylines. Two tips: clean the soil from each peg as you take them out with the point of another peg already held in the hand as a kind of dagger. Any peg which proves difficult to pull out can often be eased upwards by hooking the notch of another peg below its head and pulling. Place the pegs into their bag as you collect them.

**Collapse the tent material**
Remove the pegs from the main guys and as the tent subsides roll up the guylines and place them on the loose fabric.

**Fold up the tent (and how to do it when wet)**

If the tent has a flysheet which fits on top (rather than being a tent which hangs under the fly) roll up the flysheet first (incidentally, doorway zips should be left unfastened before folding and rolling a tent tightly). Then fold up the tent by pulling the centre ridge of the roof taut before folding everything carefully back in the same way you first opened it out.

If the base of the groundsheet is dirty, clean it with a sponge or cloth and avoid letting it come into contact with the tent material. Slip the poles into their own bag, or pack them with the tent, whichever is the case so that everything finishes up in one carrying bag.

One last point regarding a wet tent. Later we see what to do when you return home. Although this should not apply to you yet—unless you just had to go out in the rain to practise pitching yours (and then, of course, you should simply leave it standing until it dries out again)—the answer is to gather it loosely and place it into its bag on its own—poles/pegs not anywhere near. A wet tent should never be rolled tightly. And a modern tent can often be so stowed by simply wrapping everything inside the nylon flysheet which you shook hard, then spreading everything out to dry later in a warm and well-ventilated room.

In really bad conditions roll up your tent in any polythene sheeting. As for finding mud all over it—you can wipe it off straight away from nylon, but leave it on canvas and brush off later.

# 6 The Indoor Camping Workshop

Packing everything ready for a camping trip can produce a feeling of panic. There just does not seem to be the room in your rucksack or bags for all that gear, yet without it how will you manage? You try to cram in sleeping bag, tent, cooker, food, fuel bottle (remembering to keep these last two apart) and all the rest of your impedimenta but find the available space is already filled up bulging to the top after only the first items mentioned! So you take everything out and start again, and still it won't fit. Yet this book has been talking of the minimum amount of camping equipment . . . It is a feeling common to everybody at some time or other from your parents, who have had to sit on suitcases bulging so fully this was the only way to get their catches snapped together, to the quartermaster of a Himalayan climbing expedition who has suffered the same anxiety pangs when the kit would seem to overflow the crates for shipment out there.

How do you start? For a beginning you might do worse than read *The Day of the Jackal* by Frederick Forsyth. It is the story of a gunman who parades his highly powered rifle and telescopic sight in front of everybody out to catch him, virtually undetected. As such it is a masterpiece of describing how to pack the very most into the very little. Rather than spoil the story of how he does it, let me put it this way . . . Supposing you had an initiative test during your school camp, one group defending a plot of rough overgrown territory, the other group trying to breach this region. If the attacking force can actually pitch a tent somewhere in that tangled mass of rocks, undergrowth, bushes, trees, bracken and overgrown lanes for one night they have won. Yet if any of them are stopped on the way in by the defenders and caught with camping gear in their possession they are 'captured' and can take no further part in the contest. So how does the eventual winner do it? Simply by pushing his bicycle past a checkpoint whose search reveals nothing except empty pockets and not even a saddlebag to search. Then in a glade among the gorse bushes as darkness falls he unpacks his camping gear. A space blanket* pressed up tight beneath the saddle by the saddle springs; a rectangle of polythene sheet just big enough to make the fly sheet of a small Timberline Tent folded tightly and slipped down the cycle frame seat tube just below where the saddle post fits (this is the same kind of shelter in fact as described in *Survival for Young People*; only it needs a thinner plastic than the 500-gauge previously recommended for the Hang Glider tent or else it would never fit inside the cycle frame); the string which pulls the tent into a ridge and is then anchored to heavy stones along the bottom edge is also packed with the polythene down the seat tubing; and in the handlebars below the fistgrips are packed away, plastic or metal cigar tubes to hold peanuts, matches, tea etc. And because everything was stowed away so neatly nobody ever suspected the secret until too late.

Follow this principle when wrapping up your gear and pushing it into rucksack, saddlebag or canoe pack. Keep everything self-contained inside the container without any clue as to the purpose of your trip.

Advertise the fact you have a new tent and sleeping bag—and you put them at risk. You have only to turn your back on them for a moment at any large railway or bus station—your tent half-hanging from beneath the rucksack flap, the sleeping bag lashed precariously elsewhere—and when you next look round one or other has been 'lifted'. If you

---

*A space rescue blanket might measure 56in × 84in of plastic film coated with aluminium. It is windproof and waterproof, and reflects back 90 per cent of your body heat when wrapped around you. One side is coloured orange to serve as distress marker, the other is silver to bounce back heat. It weighs about three ounces, packs as small as a deck of cards and has saved lives in emergency. And on a warm night it could be used as a sleeping bag. (However, its general use is not as rugged as the strong polythene survival bag described in Chapter 2.) Optimus make such a protective sheet called Bodyguard.

are hitch hiking, there are further snags with badly packed gear. Mugs, training shoes and musical instruments hanging from the exterior of your pack frame are just the very things to put drivers off stopping for you. Pots and pans similarly attached will drive you mad with their clanking, the way they swing like pendulums and they catch on the seats and racks of public transport. Badly-arranged bundles are bad news on private transport too, especially when they fall apart during the journey!

Storing your kit compactly and neatly, however, means you must know how everything works, where it all fits and where exactly you are going. To this end you should first put it together in the 'workshop' of your home. Then, having tried the crucial aspects of lightweight camping under a safe roof, you can concentrate on getting all your camping belongings into the smallest possible space for the Big Outdoors.

## PRINTED CIRCUIT-TYPE THINKING TESTS (ON HOW EVERYTHING WORKS IN FIRST TIME LIGHTWEIGHT CAMPING)

The ultimate condensing of a lot into a little must be with space age techno-tricks like the microdot as used by secret agents (a page of this book could be reduced to the size of a pinprick, and then magnified back to be perfectly legible), the electronic chip which gives the time-read out of a digital watch (the chip being a tiny miracle made of silicon) and the printed circuit of your transistor radio (where wires and terminals are replaced by a plastic wafer traced with a metallic cobweb along which the current from the battery runs). The fact, however, that everything is so small does not mean it is necessarily also simple. There is much more to these wonders than meets the eye. And it is the same with camping.

The simplest sounding things can give you problems on first acquaintance. How, for instance, do you climb in and out of a sleeping bag the correct way? How do you light and rev up a Optimus stove? And these are only two examples. There are others. In each case, however, the answer comes first in knowing how everything works. Work on it now in that indoor workshop at home.

## Blueprint planning

When and where to go? *When* is easy: during spring, summer or autumn, but not winter. And when the weather forecast promises settled conditions. *Where* is rather more tricky, but the main rule is do not be too ambitious at first. The area you choose may be a long way from home—five or six miles a day, say, if you are walking or canoeing. And no more than four times this amount on your bike for the first time. Later, as you grow stronger and more experienced, increase these distances by all means, but remember that even for an adult backpacker 10–15 miles in a day is good going.

First, borrow guidebooks of the area you fancy from your public library. Then go over them with the appropriate Ordnance Survey sheets. Work out a day-by-day itinerary and approximate camp sites for the evenings. Do this by looking at the map and using the symbols to identify possible sites where it is possible to find shelter for your tent by hedges, walls, knolls and so on. And where streams promise fresh running water. Many farms have suitable places for camping, but be ready for a refusal and have other possible sites at your fingertips. There is also the possibility you will have to camp on an organised site in those touristic areas mentioned at the start of this book. Meanwhile the following notes may help.

## Planning backpacking tours

Try making a route card detailing each leg of your trip (as described in my book, *Climbing for Young People*). You need only do a few miles each day at this stage, remember. An adult will find 10–15 miles good going indeed when carrying a pack as well. An advantage of the route card is you can leave a copy with your parents or some other responsible adult so that people know where you are going. Choose short walks along footpaths, well-signposted and in attractive countryside as listed in the AA-Reader's Digest *No Through Road*. You can check this in your local library, and OS maps as well. Look for footpaths which are marked by a dotted line, and stick to them.

## Bicycle tour planning

Obtain a map of the country from a service station, and you now have a map of the roads to avoid. However, old roads which are parallel to motorways are fine for a bike. Aim to keep well clear of busy roads though. Hilly roads deep in the countryside make the scenery, and the Ordnance Survey 1:50,000 maps will help you plan such routes in advance as they give a clear indication of inclines—just check the contours.

## Canoe camping planning

This has already been stressed in Chapter 4. However, the largest scale map you can find for the river you intend voyaging the better. This will give more detail on the waterway itself—such as warnings of sharp bends and stepping stones and so on.

And how do you reach your camping area in the first place? Express coach or train are logical, and you can take your bicycle on the train free (in the guard's van). Hitchhiking is a standard way too for the older young person. Younger young people will need to go with parents or some other older responsible 'guardian', however, and the trip will often be by car.

The following addresses will help you find sites and suggest routes too (do send a SAE, however):

BACKPACKERS CLUB: E. Gurney, 20 St Michaels Road, Tilehurst, Reading.

BRITISH CANOE UNION: 70 Brompton Road, London SW3

CAMPING CLUB OF GREAT BRITAIN AND IRELAND LTD: 11 Lower Grosvenor Place, London SW1

CYCLISTS' TOURING CLUB: Cotterell House, 69 Meadrow, Godalming, Surrey.

THE FORESTRY COMMISSION: (for information on forest camp sites): 231 Corstophine Road, Edinburgh.

RAMBLERS' ASSOCIATION: 1/4 Crawford Mews, York Street, London W1.

YOUTH CAMPING ASSOCIATION OF GREAT BRITAIN & IRELAND: 91 Hurst Drive, Waltham Cross, Herts.

### Choosing your task force

The older person who enjoys camping, or who has never camped but would like to try, is the ideal guide to go with young people on their first camping trips. And in many cases the older person will be the one likely to have a car. Older young people grouping together is the alternative, and four is the best number. This gives two people to a tent—a good combination. Three should be looked on as the least number that is safe when venturing off the beaten track—like a backpacking or canoe trek, for instance. In which case one tent would shelter the group at a pinch.

THE REASON WHY THREE IS THE MINIMUM 'MUST' IS IN CASE OF AN ACCIDENT. ONE PERSON CAN GO FOR HELP WHILE ONE STAYS WITH THE CASUALTY—PRESUMING THERE IS ONLY ONE CASU-ALTY. HOWEVER THIS MEANS YOUR 'TASK FORCE' IS STRETCHED TO THE LIMIT IF IN FACT MORE WERE INJURED IN THE FIRST PLACE OR THE MESSENGER WAS HURT GOING FOR HELP. THERE-FORE FOUR IS BEST: TWO CAN GO FOR HELP AND ONE STAYS BEHIND TO HELP THE CASUALTY. AND IN THE CASE WHERE TWO ARE INJURED—AN UNLIKELY OCCURRENCE BUT STILL POSSIBLE—YOU STILL HAVE A MESSENGER AND A FIRST-AIDER.

The fact you persuade friends to accompany you means a lot. But forget those who are not prepared to fit in, and who are likely to turn awkward when tired or things go wrong. They will spoil it for the rest of you. Below are listed more organisations where camping is part of the routine, and you can join in.

FOREST SCHOOL CAMPS: 3 Pine View, Fairmile Park Road, Cobham, Surrey.

THE GIRL GUIDES ASSOCIATION: 17 Buckingham Palace Road, London SW1.

OUTWARD BOUND TRUST: 34 The Broadway, London SW1

THE SCOUT ASSOCIATION: Baden Powell House, Queen's Gate, London SW7.

SPORTS COUNCIL OF GREAT BRITAIN: 70 Brompton Road, London SW3.

WOODCRAFT FOLK: 13 Ritherton Road, London SW17.

## The indoor camping workshop tooling-up list

You are now ready to pack away your equipment, some of which is new, the rest being items you already have at home. Your key tool at the moment, however, is something you will not be packing—a spring balance.

Some campers go to an awful lot of trouble cutting down the weight of every item to the minimum—like sawing off the handles of toothbrushes, taking the labels off the clothing they pack and wiping every speck of soot off stoves. While it is true that every extra ounce you carry on foot makes progress that bit harder, you don't have to go to quite such extremes. But the idea still is to pack the very least number of items you can, then make the most of them.

Below is a list of essentials with their weights—as an example. These are essential items and any other accessories you carry must also be as light as possible. How you split these between your group is up to you. But at this stage nobody should carry more than 20lbs if at all possible, and 25lbs is the very most and only to be carried by the strongest group member. (Remember the rule of carrying no more pounds than the years in your age; invaluable when you are still young.)

## Twenty essentials of your kit and specimen weights

|  | lbs | oz |
|---|---|---|
| Rucksack | 3 | 01 |
| Food per person per day | 2 | |
| Tent, poles, pegs, guylines | 3 | 08 |
| Tent repair kit (adhesive tape) | 0 | 02 |
| Sleeping bag & stuff sack | 2 | 13 |
| Insulating pad | 0 | 08 |
| Stove, fuel, lighter, matches | 1 | 13 |
| Pans, billy, handle, mug, bowl | 2 | 09 |
| KFS & can opener | 0 | 06 |
| Water bottle | 0 | 01 |
| Torch, spare batteries, bulb | 0 | 10 |
| Compass, maps | 0 | 05 |
| Whistle | 0 | 01 |
| First aid kit | 0 | 08 |

Towel & soap & toilet paper ........... 0  14
Waterproof cagoule or anorak .......... 1  02
Overtrousers (waterproof) .............. 0  07
Spare clothing ........................ 4  00
Bivi bag ............................. 0  08
Sponge .............................. 0  01

If you are improvising on early trips as suggested in the chart of Chapter 4, some of your gear will be much heavier than the items listed here; a blanket sleeping bag, for instance. In that case you need to compensate by reducing the weight of other items; food, for instance. You just carry enough for one or two days rather than for more and instead buy the rest as you go. You can also adjust the weight carried by each group member so that in the end it all levels out for everyone.

With the other items not on the ESSENTIAL list, there is always the problem of what and what not to pack in the final analysis. When in doubt therefore follow this rule: *lay out everything you think you need on the floor and picture yourself using it on a really hot day (and remove the items you would not then need to reduce the weight); now imagine yourself with the remaining gear in a Cairngorm blizzard (and replace those pieces of equipment needed to survive the white-out); finally, leave out those items which would not really have helped in either example.*

### How to bench test your sleeping bag
The only workbench needed here is your insulating pad laid out on the bedroom floor. Or, if you have still to buy one of those mats, strip the covers off your bed mattress and use your sleeping bag on that. And place a sweater inside a tee-shirt as your pillow. Take the bag from its stuff sack and shake it out to fluff up the filling inside.

Climb into the bag by sitting on the mattress, knees tucked up and pull the loose bag in a ruck up to your knees. Then straighten the legs and pull the bag up in one go as far as your backside. Your feet should be touching the bottom of the bag as you continue to pull up the material until, lifting your behind, you haul up the bag around your waist. Now lie back down again, pulling the bag up round your shoulders.

Climbing out of a sleeping bag is the exact opposite. You push it down your body to your feet, and step out of it—rather like taking a sock off. Forget about climbing out of the bag as you might climb out of bed. That way will take ages.

There are two more things: to turn over inside a sleeping bag, turn over with bag, actually holding the material by your face with your hands so it is pulled taut as you turn; and stuff your bag back into the stuff sack—don't try to roll it or fold it first.

**Make an old down-filled sleeping bag almost as new**

Someone offers to lend you a sleeping bag. Only it looks so grubby the idea of sleeping inside it does not really appeal. Yet it can be cleaned quickly, and the process is valuable for when you eventually own a sleeping bag and need to clean it from time to time. Wipe off small marks with a damp cloth and Stergene first. To handwash the complete bag, however, use warm water and a soap product (NOT detergent). And be sure to handle the material gently. Rinse well and gently squeeze out most of the water. Now be really careful when handling the material as wet down is very heavy and places a lot of strain on the seams. Dry as quickly as possible with an air blower or tumble dryer; the bag must not stay wet. As it becomes dryer, shake it occasionally to spread around any bunches and clumps of down, then leave it until completely dry.

A further tip. Always keep a down-filled bag bone dry (and inside a polythene bag as well as the stuff sack it comes inside). Store in a dry cupboard folded loose rather than compressed inside that stuff sack.

## THE PESSIMIST'S GUIDE TO THE OPTIMUS

Every enthusiast of the Big Outdoors should be able to work the Optimus 96 stove (yes, the basic Primus) although they may own a different kind of cooker. Like learning to swim, riding a bike, or driving a car, you never forget, nor know when it will come in useful. What better way to learn than on a workbench?

This Optimus comes in bits and has to be assembled partly with a spanner, and by pushing other pieces together like Lego. Do this now outdoors as you are about to 'rev' your cooker like a motor bike engine: you bring it up to full throttle burning, then slacken off until it is only idling. Then boost it once again. It is not as pointless as it sounds. Cooking on a Primus includes a lot of revving up when you want water bubbling fast, say, and also some slacking off as when you want food to simmer on a low flame. The purpose of this experiment is to go about everything the wrong way, then put it right. Although this would be risky indoors, it is not when tried outdoors with plenty of space around you.

The diagram illustrates very roughly this cooking motor (because that is how it feels when roaring so fast the top glows red and the air trembles all around). How it works is simple. The paraffin in the partly-filled fuel tank is put under pressure when you replace the filler cap and screw up the air valve on top, and then begin to pump (see illustration). On pumping air into the space above the fuel, the pressure forces the paraffin up the central tube which descends almost to the bottom of the tank. When the stove is working the vaporiser is so hot that the paraffin literally boils inside it and passes eventually to the jet as a highly inflammable vapour. And it is this white gas streaming out of the jet which mixed with air burns so fiercely under the flat metal flame spreader which sits just above.

How the raw paraffin liquid is turned into vapour which burns fiercely rather than simply issues out as a fountain of flaming paraffin is the crux of learning how to use an Optimus, and why it is not simply a switch-on-switch-off machine. It has in fact to be 'primed'. At the base of the vaporiser tube fits the narrow circular dish which you fill with meths (or Meta solid-fuel tablets broken up small or burning paste). When this is lit the flames heat the vaporiser tube so that paraffin which passes up the inside is heated and becomes vapour. And that is what burns furiously when it reaches the open air.

That is the theory. Now let's put everything together on the top of a low wall, box or old table outside. Stand the fuel tank on its three short legs firmly, then attach the vaporiser tube,

priming dish burner head and flame spreader to the tank—
using a spanner carefully to screw the tube to the tank (NOT
too hard or you might damage the threads). Then position the
three cooking support legs which slide into metal sleeves on the
side of the tank and you are almost ready for blast-off. But
during your count-down remember . . .

LIGHT THE STOVE BY FILLING THE FUEL TANK, AND UN-
FASTENING THE AIR VALVE ON THE TANK. NOW FILL THE PRIMING
DISH AND LIGHT THAT. WAIT AS THE FLAMES HEAT UP THE
VAPORISER TUBE AND THEN CLOSE THE AIR VALVE. PUSH THE
FUEL TANK PUMP SEVERAL TIMES AS THE PRIMING FUEL FLAMES
DIE DOWN AND THE STOVE SHOULD ROAR INTO LIFE.

### You pumped and pumped and nothing happened
Shake the fuel tank. Hear anything? If not it is either empty or
too full. It should be no more than two thirds full when you
start.

### You tried again. Still nothing.
The nozzle on top of the vaporiser tube is probably blocked.
So take one of the thin wire prickers which come with the stove
and probe the tiny aperture so it is clean and open. (AND
always carry spare prickers in the stove box for when this
happens).

### This time you pumped and a flaming paraffin gusher shot into the sky
The rule is: hands off the pump UNTIL the priming fuel is
almost finished. You must wait until the flames around the
vaporiser tube have almost died down, then—and only
then—close up the air valve and give the pump a pump.

### You did this, and still fiery paraffin flew up again
You pumped too hard. It must be gentle pumping, just several
short jabs on the pump (and when you know your stove it
might just start with two or three) until you feel the resistance
of the pressure building up inside.

**Each time the paraffin flamed you did not know what to do**

Simply release the air valve and the pressure inside the fuel tank eases off so the flames die down.

Practised Optimus owners, in fact, let a wet paraffin gusher, once started, subside until it has almost disappeared; then screw up the air valve once more and pump gently. There is a chance then they may just catch some vaporised paraffin emerging. If not you need reach for meths (or Meta fuel or burning paste) and matches and start all over again.

**You've got it! The stove roars into action with first an orange flame around the flame spreader which then turns blue. And then suddenly the gusher shoots up once more . . .**

Overpumping again. Once the Primus is burning it only needs the occasional pump to maintain its heat. To increase power let it rev on a while longer before increasing the pressure, and then only a pump stroke or two at a time.

**You singe—OUCH!—a finger priming the stove**

Watch burning meths—or rather, watch out. Its flame is invisible a lot of the time, and there is a risk that if you were to bring an Optimus into the tent the meths could set light to your shelter even before the stove was properly lit. Only cook outside therefore.

**You have the stove roaring at full blast now through gradually and correctly increasing the pressure, only you then want to lower the temperature by unscrewing the air valve and it goes out . . .**

Right idea, but be a bit smarter about closing up the air valve again after unscrewing it. Sometimes you can catch the stove at the last second by pumping as you screw up the valve. When, however, you have tightened up the valve and still the stove has gone out you can still light it again if you are quick. A lighter or a match flame put to the nozzle at the top of the vaporiser tube will catch hot paraffin vapour still emerging and start the stove immediately.

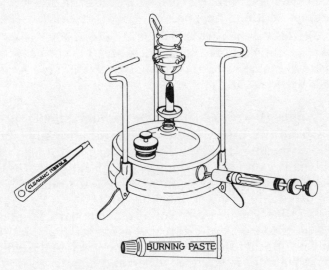

*The Workshop Optimus Test Rig*

**The priming flame blew everywhere in a breeze; and so did the flame around the flame spreader when the stove was going**

A windshield to fit around the vaporiser tube helps. Use this. To shield the top of the stove as well—a large rock or similar object will do. Some people hang a small asbestos blanket on the windy side of the stove, but it is one extra item to pack.

**By this time you ran out of the small bottle of meths you used for priming (or the small box of solid fuel or tube of burning paste)**

Now is the time to practise what you would do in camp were the same thing to happen . . . Close up the valve first, then twist up a small piece of paper and jam it into the priming dish. Build up the pressure pumping gently until raw paraffin fountains from the nozzle and spills down the sides of the vaporiser tube on to the paper. Now undo the air valve, light the paper and carry on as you did before. Its disadvantage is that it is messy.

**The Optimus you borrowed just won't raise the pressure when you pump—nothing happens**

Unscrew the pump part and look at the washer (like on a bicycle pump). You may need a new one, but the chances are that rubbing margerine or cooking fat on it as a lubricant will make it work again.

**The Optimus (borrowed still) came without a flame spreader**

Simply bend two prickers across the space normally taken by the flame spreader. It serves the same purpose for now. If you were actually camping, anything of a similar shape to the flame spreader would do as well—say a small flat stone.

Primus cooking may seem—after all this—to be so tricky that it will be beyond you. Not at all. The paraffin pressure stove is as docile as a powerful car—so long as you practise like this at first. Rather than being under-powered and needing to be coaxed along, it has the power and simply needs to be handled with respect.

## TUNE UP YOUR TRANGIA

The alternative young person's cooker is the meths storm stove, and the Trangia is—like the Optimus paraffin stove— the basic kind. Or you might instead buy the Fjallraven or the Optimus 77A. It's still the same difference. Much simpler to operate than the Optimus (although not as fast-cooking nor as cheap to run nor as adjustable for the flame either), these cookers are used increasingly by outdoor pursuits centres like Outward Bound schools. They can be used in a howling wind too, although the more shelter you find obviously the better for then your stove does not gulp the fuel down quite as quickly.

The stove comes complete with the pots and pans mentioned in Chapter 4. Begin by undoing the strap which surrounds the frying pan and windshield section into which everything is packed, and lift out the bits and pieces inside: the frying pan itself, the bulldog-type pan gripper, the cooking pot, the small kettle, the meths burner (wrapped in a plastic bag inside the kettle) and the other half of the wind guard.

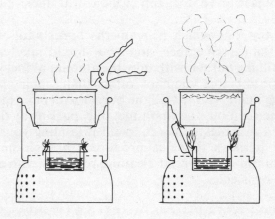

*The Trangia's Two-Speed Controller*

Next, fit the two parts of the wind guard together. The hooks on the upper part should be checked next; fold them up as a support when the frying pan is used; fold them down, however, when using the pot or kettle for boiling. The frying pan can also be used as a lid. Turned upside down and place it over a pan heating on the cooker (to make the warming quicker).

Take the burner, flip up the low-flame flanged rim which fits around the top, unscrew the top and fill the burner no more than two thirds full of meths. This should last nearly half an' hour's burning time and—after placing the burner in its aperture inside the windshield—you can practise both simmering and boiling a potful of water for a mug of tea. After the Optimus, this is simplicity itself: hinge the low-flame rim upwards for full-speed burning, but place it down over the flame when you want things to simmer on only a low heat.

To extinguish your cooker, place the low-flame rim down, wait until the flame is only just showing then place a tin can or similar object over the top which will then cut it out completely.

And a few tips which help: meths burns with an almost invisible flame, remember, and you should take care when lighting; fill the burner with only the amount of fuel you think you will need before you cook rather than topping it up each time to the limit; NEVER fill the burner with more meths until it has gone right out the first time; only pack away the burner empty and in a plastic bag to avoid it tainting your cooking gear; the burner's flame is produced through small holes around its rim—these need cleaning regularly with a piece of thin wire or needle.

ALTHOUGH A PETROL STOVE WORKS LIKE A PRIMUS—YOU CLOSE THE AIR VALVE AND JAB THE PUMP TO BUILD UP PRESSURE BEFORE APPLYING A MATCH—YOU DO NOT NEED METHS OR SOLID FUEL TO PRIME IT. USE INSTEAD THE PETROL ITSELF AS THE STARTER. HOWEVER DO BE CAREFUL, EVEN THOUGH ONLY A SMALL AMOUNT IS INVOLVED. USE A PRICKER OFTEN TO KEEP THE NOZZLE FREE FROM BLOCKS. AND KEEP THE COOKER WELL AWAY FROM ANYTHING WHICH COULD CATCH FIRE.

## Fuelling safety rules for filling a stove

Whichever your type of stove, be sure you know how to operate it correctly and watch the following safety points in the first place. *Refuel* your stove away from the tent (and outside your house right now) and never near a naked flame; A *burning stove* should never be left unattended; *spare fuel* should always be kept outside the tent and away from the stove (again, outside your house, please); A *windshield* is a necessary accessory and be sure that your stove is standing firmly at all times (and especially when lighting it); *Gas cylinders—if* your stove runs off this fuel—should be changed with special care, and the empty cylinders kept outside your tent.

## WORKSHOP COOKING REPAIRS

Practise cooking in your kitchen or in the backyard so you eat meals actually prepared on your Optimus or meths storm stove rather than on the electric or North Sea gas cooker. Use only the same ingredients you plan to eat camping. And the menus too. Then watch out for where cooking repairs are needed.

Burnings, boilings-over and other disasters will have to be mended on the spot, each one giving you experience so the same mistakes are rather less likely to happen again. That they are not as serious in the safety of your home does not mean you should take them any the less lightly out of doors. You might be miles from a shop, say, and tip over your entire evening meal as it comes to the boil—well, that's dangerous when there is no other food. A warm evening meal is a vital part of camping whatever your activity. And so you are in fact learning the safe way to cook as much as aiming for great-tasting meals.

The fact you will only be using a couple of pots and one burner means that everything must be kept simple. Forget ambitious meals. Concentrate on the quickest and most economical sequence of using your pans instead. Use only the foods you like best—baked beans and sausages, for instance, if that is your favourite. In the Big Outdoors the only real limitation on your cooking is that your appetite will be too keen to want to wait long for a meal. You want food fast and hot, and nothing fancy.

Food that may be easy to eat at home might not necessarily be the same in camp—from cornflakes which blow away in the wind to bread which falls apart when wet. Think in terms of camping convenience first therefore, and buy your food with that in mind.

The actual cooking should be easy. Just follow the instructions on the labels of the food you buy. Where none exist, now is your chance to learn how to fry bacon or boil an egg at home. You will quickly learn, for instance, the two ways of preparing food on your single-burner . . .

That BOILING (or STEWING) is generally your easiest way as several ingredients can be cooked together in the same pot, even if they have to be added at different times—for instance, you would add brussels sprouts to a pan of potatoes towards the end of the boiling time of the potatoes as the sprouts only take around five minutes to do. Fast boiling water is no more efficient than quietly boiling water, and it uses up fuel a lot faster. And a third thing you will find is that the hot water from boiling is a spin-off for washing up too.

And you will discover that FRYING is the quickest way (where food is heated on one side at a time in shallow fat like margerine or cooking fat). However, fierce frying is not advised; it makes meat tough and shrinks it in size. So forget about fat so hot it gives off blue smoke unless sealing meat or potatoes in the first few seconds before adjusting the flame to allow the food to cook at a slower rate with a quiet sizzle (and no smoke). You will also find no doubt that it is not a good idea to crack eggs on the side of the frying pan actually on the cooker as you then upset the lot—cooker, pan and all; instead rap the egg on some other edge and pour into the pan.

EAT A BREAKFAST THAT IS QUICK AS YOU LIE INSIDE YOUR SLEEPING BAG, THEN FORTIFY YOUR STRENGTH DURING THE DAY BY CHEWING ENERGY FOODS LIKE CHOCOLATE, SWEETS, SALTED PEANUTS, RAISINS, KENDAL MINT CAKE, FLAPJACK, DATES, FIGS OR PEANUT BUTTER SANDWICHES. THIS KIND OF NOSH (ALONG WITH DRINKS OF COLD WATER) WILL KEEP YOU GOING UNTIL EVENING AND THERE IS NO NEED FOR A SET LUNCH AS A RESULT. HOT SUPPER IS MOST NECESSARY, HOWEVER, AND SHOULD BE AS SIMPLY AND QUICKLY MADE AS WAS BREAKFAST (AND IN FACT THOSE MEALS YOU PREPARED ON YOUR FIRST NIGHT OUT AT THE START OF THE BOOK).

It cannot be stressed enough how recipes should be simple and quick to do. And the things you like to eat rather than what anyone says you *should*. Your breakfast, for example, doesn't even *have* to be heated. Just muscle-up some muesli with Horlicks, grated chocolate, brown sugar and dried milk and you feel the good it does you inside. As for supper, it could be made like this . . .

Take a packet of soup, follow the instructions and heat it in a pan. As the soup starts to bubble beef it up with some tinned milk; a spoonful or two of porridge; a handful of potato flakes or powder; a little curry powder; a few slices of luncheon meat or corned beef or tinned steak; a slice or two of apple; a date or two; some salt; dried onion flakes; slices of cheese; anything else you fancy. It tastes better than it looks, and you can finish off with fruit and coffee.

THROUGH ALL THIS YOU WILL HAVE BEEN USING TAP WATER AT HOME. WHAT OF THE WATER, HOWEVER, ONLY AVAILABLE AT YOUR CAMP SITES? MOST STREAM WATER RUNNING DOWN SLOPES IS DRINKABLE WHEN MOVING—THAT IS, NOT LOCKED IN STAGNANT POOLS. THE SAFEST RULE, HOWEVER, IS TO BOIL IT FIRST. THEN YOU CAN CARRY IT WITH YOU IN LOWLAND AREAS WHERE CLEAN WATER MAY NOT BE SO PLENTIFUL. THIS IS GENERALLY UNNECESSARY IN HILL REGIONS OR DISTRICTS WHERE HEAVY RAINFALL IS NORMAL (EXCEPT IN PROLONGED DRY PERIODS, OR LIMESTONE AND CHALK AREAS). THE THING IS THAT A PINT OF WATER WEIGHS 1¼lbs. THERE IS NO POINT IN CARRYING IT AROUND MUCH OF THE COUNTRYSIDE.

## Washing up, washing and the washing try-outs

Instead of carrying detergent, soap flakes and the bathroom sink let nature do much of the cleaning in camp for you. Your cooking utensils—KFS, kitchen-drawer-out-of—for instance, should not be cleaned in the kitchen sink now but in your backyard or garden. This also goes for washing up pots you have cooked with on your stove and any clothes you need to clean at the moment.

Take a bucketful of cold water outside to stand in for the water you would normally find in a camp site stream. You also need one cooking pan full of hot water (which on a camp site would have been heating up as you drank that last mug of coffee).

To wash dirty pots and pans, KFS and so on, you need a small area of soil. In the country you could dig this out with a penknife—then cover it afterwards with the sod you removed. For now, though, any soil will do (and you can cover it with fresh soil afterwards). Now fill one dirty pan with cold water from the bucket and clean around it by rubbing the metal with a bunch of grass. Pour the mucky water into the next pan or on to some other utensil in need of cleaning and loosen the dirt on that too. Then fill the original pan with more clean water to give a final rinse.

You will discover that so long as the pan was not greasy or

had food burnt to it, you could clean it this way. If it had been used for frying, however, or had burnt food stuck to it, you would find the cold water made things even messier. So use instead a little of the hot water you brought in the pan. Then you can wipe out the grease with handfuls of grass (or on the camp site with ferns, leaves, reeds etc), and then swill out everything with cold water.

Mud and small pebbles are a good scouring agent for removing grease. Just stick dirty knives and forks into the ground, for instance, pull them out and polish them on the grass until they shine. Scrape off burnt food first with a sharp stone.

ONE WORD HERE, HOWEVER. PIECES OF VEGETATION USED AS PAN SCRUBBERS SHOULD BE DUG BACK INTO THE SOIL AFTERWARDS— IN THE PLACE WHERE YOU POURED THE DIRTY WATER ALONG WITH DEBRIS FROM DIRTY PLATES. NEVER POUR THIS ON TO GRASS OR BACK INTO STREAMS SO THE MUCK SETTLES ON THE STREAM OR RIVERBED.

Washing yourself with the minimum of hot water can be tried standing in the bath. Just take one potful of hot water, a piece of soap, your camping sponge and a towel. Ready? You are about to use the same principle as you did for washing up: to use a little warm water to loosen the dirt, then unlimited cold water to swill it all away.

Take off your clothes, place the pan at your feet, soap up the sponge and begin to wash from the head—working downwards. Top up the pot as you do the second going-over yourself—so you now have a lukewarm solution for more actual washing. Finish by rinsing yourself with cold water from the sponge.

Mud is a good soap if you need to get rid of dirt and grease, and have nothing else. Use plenty of elbow grease as you rub your skin and it will come fairly clean.

And washing clothes? Try this in the bathroom, too. A couple of dirty shirts will give you all the experience you need. Soak them first for half an hour in a pan of hot water in which you have stirred a few shavings from a bar of soap. Then rub the actual soap cake into the places where dirt shows like collar and cuffs and rinse well in cold water. You can do this by alternately swishing and squeezing the garments in a stream. Spread the garments out to dry in the sun. But if you had to move on to another camp site and the cloth was still damp, carry in a plastic bag.

## QUARTZ DIGITAL WRISTWATCH-TYPE PACKING-A-LOT-INTO-A-LITTLE SYSTEMS

Press the button on your digital watch and the red figures glow as if car brakes have been stamped on. Yet how much is packed away in that small pack on your wrist from the tiny electrical battery to the miracle quartz chip. And everything has its place.

This is how your rucksack or pack frame should be filled. And your cycle bags and canoe packs too. When everything is fitted inside as firmly as a Cumberland pork sausage you have got it right. None of the seams overstrained, yet none too slack either. Now in your workshop is the place to practise packing the ingredients you have finally brought together. If you have followed the advice so far it is just a matter of fitting it all inside in the right order now.

### How to make any pack look as good as an outdoor shop window rucksack galaxy

Rucksacks, pack frames and even small day sacks look great on the shop shelf—as firmly bulging as if blown up with hydrogen and ready to float away (despite their price tags which soon bring you back to earth). What happens when you get the pack home, however? Often you will find it is too large for your requirements—say, when you are only going for a day's hike from your tent which is being used as a base camp and you are consequently not carrying anything more on your back than a spare sweater, anorak, food, first-aid kit and map and compass. The pack will then look as good as a deflated balloon. So how do the shops make rucksacks 'look good' in the first place?

The secret is in a sheet of thin insulating foam pad which is trimmed with a sharp knife so that it completely lines the pack except for where it rests against your back. As the diagram shows, it is easily made, and serves another purpose besides simply 'bellying' out your pack to look OK.

It lets you see what you are doing. Normally the mouth of a rucksack closes together after you push each piece of kit inside and you have to open it up again to look where the next item goes. This way, with a thin lining of plastic foam, however, you can see inside the bag all the time.

The system can also be used for cycle bags and canoe packs. And of course all the pieces of insulating pad used can be pieced together to give under-the-sleeping-bag insulation in camp.

### How to pack your rucksack

Pack your rucksack with care. Heavy items like the tent go on top; lightweight ones, like sleeping bags, at the bottom. There is more to it than this, however.

First, line the rucksack with a large bag made from strong 500-gauge polythene (as well as the insulating pad liner). This will then save the contents when out in heavy rain, or if your pack falls into water. Then wrap certain other items in individual plastic bags—like food, sleeping bag, cooker and fuel bottle. And spare clothes too. The more polythene bags you have in camp the better, as they have so many uses—like wrapping up wet clothing.

Now push the sleeping bag into the bottom of the rucksack. Immediately the space inside will seem to have shrunk by half! The answer is to press a stockinged foot down on top and push hard while at the same time pulling the edges of the rucksack upwards. Spare clothing can now be packed both down the back of the sack where your spine will rub while walking, and also—if necessary—on top of the sleeping bag. Again, really press everything into place squeezing hard. Laying the rucksack on its back will help to arrange this padding.

The rest of the space inside is now taken up with—stove, fuel bottle, cooking utensils, food and sponge. A lot of space can be saved by 'nesting' gear inside hollow objects such as cooking pots, training shoes and mug. Stuff smaller items inside them. And at the top, the tent, which should fit snugly below the top flap. Items like cagoule or anorak can also fit into the top or be worn around the waist, sleeves knotted in a reef knot in front. Gloves and hat and waterproof pants can

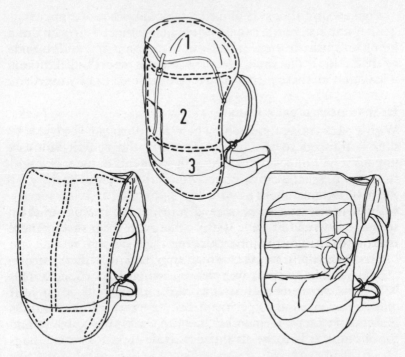

*The Boiled Sweet Jar Rucksack Packing System*
*In top rucksack, 1. is for heavy items 2. for medium weight and*
*3. for Lightweight*

also be packed away here. Items like map and compass, money, torch, first-aid kit and camera, however, are best kept inside the zipped compartment inside the top flap, or actually on your person. Then they can be reached quickly whenever you need them.

Packing can be simplified by using plastic sweet bottles as suggested for canoeing. The tops can be cut off the bottles just below the neck and these prove ideal containers for smaller objects; even when empty they still preserve the shape of the sack to look as if it is full. Or you can leave the bottle tops on.

This explains the packing of a one-bag rucksack (the type climbers prefer), but supposing there are outside pockets on the bag? And supposing your rucksack is in fact a pack frame where the sack rests on its frame?

Pockets on either side of a rucksack have the advantage that cooker and fuel bottle can be stored inside them—so keep these items well away from the food (not to mention sleeping bag and spare clothes). The smell of fuel permeates everything if there is a leak and all these pieces of gear are jammed tightly together.

### How to pack a pack frame

With a pack frame the sleeping bag can be attached outside the sack—strapped to the frame. This has the benefit you can unpack it without ever disturbing the contents of the sack itself. It is not an essential advantage. Mountaineers, who have by far the most exhausting of any rucksack-carrying activity, survive with their sleeping bags packed away in the bottom of their sacks, and wouldn't have it any other way. They dislike pack frames for being ungainly, catching the wind and having too many corners and pockets which they reckon unnecessary.

Apart from a sleeping bag possibly being attached separately below the pack, do not attach anything else outside; keep it hidden inside. And experiment until everything has its right place inside there. Remember to wrap sleeping bag in a waterproof bag if it is to be strapped outside the rucksack.

### How to pack a day sack on the sweet-jar-stuff-sack principle

The rucksack used as a 'day' sack for short hikes and rambles should have extra packing inside as well as the layer of closed-cell insulating pad already described. Otherwise it flaps about on your back mostly empty. The essentials for such a trip are quite few; food, flashlight, map and compass, spare sweater or two, bivi bag and waterproofs. However you can also fill empty space with plastic sweet bottles—as detailed in Chapter 4—with or without their tops cut off. The point being, even empty they will pack your rucksack so it keeps its shape. And you will be able to pack some of your gear inside them too. In fact most of it.

### Two tips for adjusting rucksacks

Rucksacks usually have a cord round the top edge of the bag so that once everything is inside it can be tightened to secure the load. Knots are out of date for this as they freeze or jam.

Instead a cord grip—worth it—is used which still holds the cord firmly in place. You press with the thumb to release the grip on the cord and pull it through. To be fully effective, however, two cords should be run through the hole and not just one. Or use a cork again.

Secondly: the buckles on many modern rucksacks tend to slip on the soapy-feeling webbing or straps so rub Copydex (liquid latex glue) on both sides of the straps. And allow to dry. You will obtain more friction this way.

### How to pack your cycle bags

It depends on your combination of bags as to what equipment goes where. A basic rule, however, is to pack tent and sleeping bag on top in the saddlebag. Food and spare clothing can then go inside panniers—front or rear, say, and the cooker and fuel in the pockets attached to the panniers (if any)—otherwise split them up to avoid any contact with your food. The side pockets on a saddlebag are also useful for this purpose. Generally, cycle campers carry less than backpackers as they are not as remote from shops and habitation.

The handlebar bag is good for items which might be needed quickly en route—like map, coins, pencil, travel tickets, lock and chain, camera, first-aid kit, batteries, spare clothing, tools, anorak, or the day's food say. Raincape and leggings are traditionally rolled and strapped on top of the saddle bag. Tent poles can also be strapped on to the rear carrier grid or across the top of the saddlebag under the flap.

### The canoe packing system

The diagram in Chapter 4 showed how supplies could be stashed inside a canoe—tent, sleeping bag and spare clothing at the stern, and food and cooking materials in the bows. This was only a suggestion, however, and you might find your kit packs better the other way round. There are two things to remember, however. The first is that you must leave the cockpit area completely free from gear—that is, the area from the footrest to the back of your seat. If you capsize there must be unrestricted space for your body to leave the cockpit under water. The other thing is that your canoe will balance best in the water with the maximum weight of your kit placed nearest the centre—hence the lightest items like sleeping bags go furthest away, say at the very stern. Lastly, when you have checked the canoe does float level, tie the bags to the small loops of nylon line 'glassed' into the canoe interior by passing a seperate piece of cord through the loop in the boat *and* the loop where the plastic of each bag is folded back at the neck with the rubber band as described in Chapter 4. And tie the the cord with a bow.

So you can pull each bag out of the canoe it also helps to have tied a retrieval line to each bag. Then, after untying the bow which holds a particular bag in place by reaching into the depths of the boat, you simply pull the line and the whole bag appears out of its usually highly inaccessible storage spot.

It is important the bags keep their position in the canoe as your first test is to check the canoe sits correctly in the water; dead-level. The gear should go fore and aft of the cockpit, and neither bows nor stern should dip further into the water than the other. Otherwise it makes paddling over a distance hard work. Also, the fact your bags are attached to your craft means they cannot come free and float away if you capsize.

# 7   All Camping Systems Go

All systems go, great . . . But go exactly where? Now is the time
to find out. Plan a very short trip with the equipment you have
begun to collect such as the new tent, Klondyke bedroll (sewn
together rather than safety-pinned) and a small solid-fuel
cooker. And travel by the means of transport most suited to
you, and preferably the most adventurous. You have a bike?
Then take a two-day spin. You would sooner canoe (and own
one)? Then paddle down your nearest stretch of safe waterway
be it canal or cascades (small ones racing through fields),
camping en route and the next day reaching the point where
parents or friends wait to pick you up with car and roofrack
(for the canoe). Or perhaps instead you carry your canoe on the
roofrack to some fabulous riverside camp site, spend the night
there, to freewheel downcurrent next morning. If hiking is your
bag, however, try backpacking for a weekend with two nights
spent on different sites. An alternative here is to pitch the tent
on one spot only, then walk each day along different routes,
returning to 'base camp' each evening.

## THE GETTING THERE AND BACK UNDER YOUR OWN STEAM

The rules of taking your tent on tour are not always obvious.
All kinds of things can go wrong before you reach the camp
site, or even prior to getting to the point from where you start
walking—as backpackers have found to their cost, for
instance, when money has been lost or stolen on coach or train.
My book, *Survival for Young People*, detailed what to do in

such crises; for now, however, keep things simple. You don't, for instance, take anything valuable with you other than essentials. A lot of money is unnecessary; so is an expensive camera at this stage.

### Travelling by the Vibram Express*

Kwells or Marzine will help you stop feeling travel sick as you go by car, coach or train en route for where you begin walking.

Keep your timetable flexible. If the weather turns wild forget your trip for now; although later in the chapter you learn how to use bad weather to good advantage, high winds and heavy rain ask too much at first, and the risk is too great. Very hot weather can be equally exhausting, and the only way here is to pitch camp early in the afternoon and walk through the cool hours of early morning through to around noon.

Avoid pushing yourself to do big mileages right now. If someone wants to brew-up along the way, or stop for a swim—do just that. You will start again feeling refreshed and more comfortable.

Respect high, remote and exposed ground which can prove dangerous at any time of year. At 500 feet a mild valley breeze becomes a freezing gale. Temperatures plummet, rain becomes torrential, mist blankets visibility and the going becomes leaden. Let the experience you gain govern your ambitions, therefore. At the greenhorn stage as you are now, keep to those regions where you are never too far from a road and habitations—something possible in many of our mountain and moorland areas (as we saw in Chapter 6). Learning from experience, for instance, can be deliberately achieved by trying the following experiments from the start. They all illuminate key 'away from home' truths.

*Boots

| NAME OF TEST AND WHAT TO DO | HOW TO TEST WHO WINS | THE PRIZE |
|---|---|---|
| **A GREYHOUND DERBY** Everyone sets out at own pace, but must keep within sight of each other for safety reasons. Anyone who, when leading, goes out of sight is disqualified. | Time limit is one hour. Anyone who stops to rest drops out. Anyone overtaken by someone they themselves had overtaken earlier after half an hour also drops out. The group gathers together after 60 minutes, then start forward again at once. Winner is one who can read without pause while walking the small print on a Mars Bar label—aloud. | Those who can talk without effort while walking are at *their* right pace. The prize being just that—the terrific ease of walking so obtained. |

THIS TEST TOOK INTO ACCOUNT THAT SOME PEOPLE ARE ALWAYS FITTER THAN OTHERS AND CAN TALK EASILY WHILE STILL WALKING FASTER. ON ACTUAL HIKES, HOWEVER, THE IDEAL PACE FOR EVERYONE IN A GROUP IS THAT OF THE SLOWEST PERSON WALKING AT THEIR BEST PACE—THAT IS, SLOWLY ENOUGH FOR THEM TO BE ABLE TO TALK AS THEY WALK.

| NAME OF TEST AND WHAT TO DO | HOW TO TEST WHO WINS | THE PRIZE |
|---|---|---|
| THE REDSKIN TRIAL At middle of day examine bare feet and dip into water (and take along Redskin Kit: UHU glue, stretch-fabric elastoplast dressing strip, scissors, and some polyurethane foam scrap). | Anyone with red skin on their heels or round their toes loses. Toenails that are too long and cutting into neighbours are also penalty-makers. Red Indians might have been stoic; you don't have to be. You should have stopped earlier to tend that sore skin—all potential blisters. | The prize for all those with white feet being the incredible comfort you win while walking compared with those whose skin is starting to rub. BOOBY PRIZE of Redskin Kit given to Losers. |

ALWAYS STOP EARLY WHENEVER YOU FEEL FEET CHAFING AND PATCH THEM UP. IF IN DOUBT—SAY BREAKING-IN NEW BOOTS— PATCH FEET WITH STRETCH FABRIC DRESSING BEFORE YOU EVEN PUT BOOTS ON. PLASTIC FOAM IS ANOTHER AID: GLUE AROUND INSIDE OF ANKLE AND BENEATH TONGUE WHEN BOOTS ARE MADE FROM UNPADDED LEATHER AND RUB IN THESE PLACES.

THE SWEATER TEST
Everyone wears cagoules
or anoraks zipped up
from start of walk—even
when day is fine and even
warm. And wear hats too.

Walk all morning. Judge by noon. Winner is the
one who fills his/her anorak so full of water on
the inside from condensation that when the
garment is squeezed there will be enough water to
mop the face, which will be very welcome at this
point.

The Prize is the
knowledge gained
by everybody who
will not wear too
much clothing
again in a hurry.

WATERPROOFS IN PARTICULAR BOTTLE BACK BODY HEAT AND ARE
REALLY OPPRESSIVE IN ANYTHING BUT WET OR COLD CONDITIONS.
NEVER WEAR LEGGINGS OR ANORAKS UNLESS ACTUALLY RAINING
OR THE WIND IS BITING THROUGH YOUR SWEATERS. TOO MANY
WALKERS WEAR TOO MUCH GEAR AND BECOME LAGGARDLY WITH-
OUT KNOWING WHY. EVEN ON A FROSTY MORNING THE BODY HEATS
UP QUICKLY AFTER YOU HAVE WALKED FOR TWENTY MINUTES OR
SO.

| NAME OF TEST AND WHAT TO DO | HOW TO TEST WHO WINS | THE PRIZE |
|---|---|---|
| **THE SORE THUMBS HITCHING TRICK** Simply watch for anyone who first of all keeps tucking thumbs below shoulder straps on his back as he walks, THEN tries pushing his pack higher up the back with his hands from below. | Rucksacks and pack frames should always be worn high on the shoulders—and if a hip belt is attached this should be fastened around the middle. Sacks slung too low rub the small of the back and the shoulders and cause aches and pains which make walking too tiring, and these two signs are clues that this is the case in your instance. | Winner is the one at the end of the day who has not needed to adjust the sack at all through the day and who has been comfortable throughout. |

STANDARD RULES IN COMFORT AND EASE OF MOVEMENT LIKE THESE ARE NOT JUST FOR YOUR ENJOYMENT BUT SAFETY TOO. SMALL THINGS CAN LEAD TO IRRITATION AND AGGRO WHICH CAN SPLIT A GROUP, ALWAYS RISKY. THE GROUP SHOULD ALWAYS STICK TOGETHER EVEN IF SOMEONE STOPS TO TIE A BOOTLACE OR TAKE A PHOTOGRAPH. OR ONE OF YOU WANTS TO GO BACK.

## Pedal-pushing tent-touring adventure

The bicycle is the fastest most efficient means yet devised for a person to move about under their own power. This goes for the one-speed bike as for the 10-speed model. The fact is you too can make easy work of covering distance as if you were always cycling down the uphill stretch of an 'Electric Brae'—the hill in Scotland where, by a freak of optical illusion, you actually freewheel up to the summit.

It does not matter how fast you go on your first camping with bicycle tour, nor how many miles you cover. If the wind is against you, forget about battling on for miles—at this stage anyway. Branch off along a road where the wind only hits you from the side. Or even stop early and camp. Never under-estimate the struggle of a day's riding into the wind when you are young; sitting exposed on a bicycle with mainly the legs working can prove a bitter experience. Rather than choose a straight line there-and-back route—and where you must face the wind coming back which was behind you going—go for triangular or D-shaped routes where you will rarely catch the wind head-on. Not that there should be any wind if the weather forecast you checked first was accurate.

## Paddling your own camping kit

Near your home, perhaps, there is a stretch of small river navigable by canoe. It is surprising how far you can journey along this river when rain brings the level an inch or two higher—though, of course, you should not venture on to water if it were to rise to a dangerous level. Travelling with the current brings ever-changing situations—and brings them quickly. You should know exactly what to do in three particular instances: how to tell when rapids or white water is ahead; how to negotiate them; what to do if you capsize.

Rapids ahead can be identified by their noise and by the quiet water just above them. Land well clear of each fall and examine it from the bank. Attempt to shoot ONLY when there are small waves, few rocks, only minute whirlpools and eddies and a clear way through. Never shoot a weir but carry your canoe round. Or, where possible with safety, float it down the water on a deckline from the bank—say, on stretches of white water you consider too risky to canoe. The same goes for any stretch of white water other than the smallest (which you can try if you feel confident and have complied with those safety rules in Chapter 4): carry the canoe round.

Below some rapids there are white waves known as 'stoppers'. These are caused by fast water hitting deep, slower channels—as when you turn a tap full force into the bath. Aim clear of all such breakers because similar-looking waves sometimes conceal rocks. Worse still—'stoppers' can literally hold you fast.

The current is your freewheel but use it carefully. Never follow it to the outside of a bend thick with willows; they will trap you. When you wish to avoid an obstacle ahead make the current do the work. The trick is known as the 'ferry glide', it is essential on the river and you should practise it whenever you are following a river current downstream. Even if you cannot do a draw stroke, telemark turn or Eskimo roll (nor have any intention of learning these more advanced techniques), you must know how to ferry glide, and break out of fast flowing water.

It is done like this. Imagine you are being swept straight for a rock or overhanging river bank by the current which is snatching you out of control. Panic as an L-driver might, and you tend to paddle faster, hoping to miss the hazard by inches. Chances are that if you do you will hit it head-on. So back-paddle HARD. And harder on the hazard side so your stern swings away from the danger although your bows point towards it. Now holding the canoe in this position by quick back-paddling strokes, the current will automatically flick you across the current and out of danger as surely as steering into it will get a car driver out of a backwheel skid.

Only practise this first in a smooth current without a weir, whirlpool, rapids waiting just downstream. And learn to ferry glide your canoe facing both up and down stream.

And if you do capsize? You will always break water close to the boat after falling out of the cockpit. Throw an arm across it—or hang on to the decklines. Get your bearings. Then swim for the nearest river bank grasping the upstream end by its toggle, but never by the small loop of rope to which the tape is attached—as was stressed before. The current will carry you downstream while doing this so keep swimming at 90 degrees to the current. The canoe's angle across the current will help ferry glide you both into the side. *Then* you can chase the paddle—if you have not already grasped it immediately on capsizing (the best plan!) and any packages that floated free. Empty out the canoe by turning it upside down and lifting the ends, straighten out the gear packed in it, patch up any holes with canoe tape, squeeze out your clothes and begin again.

## FINDING A PITCH

Look for your camp site in good time, first spotting a really nice area to spend the night and then stopping at the first farm and asking permission (or where permission can be obtained). Realise that you may have to ask several farmers before you are granted that permission, and it will save you a lot of anxiety. That is why, of course, you should start searching for a pitch well before it gets dark. If canoeing, say, do not paddle on into the middle of a town as sun goes down. There will be no camp sites at all here, or you may have to camp on a municipal camp site. This means pushing on downstream for another mile or two to be away from sewage, rubbish and factory-polluted scenery and water.

Go about asking for permission to camp the right way. If, for instance, your friends start pitching the tents as you go to ask at the farm—possible trouble! Instead, brew up tea while someone goes to the farm; at least if you are turned down the drink will revive you. Keep things simple when asking too. Requests for milk and eggs are not always popular; on the other hand you may be offered them *and* shelter in a barn if it is raining hard. Only never take it for granted you will always be so welcome. The only stipulation you might make is that you are not put in a field where there are cows, pigs, horses and any other possible threats to tents.

### Shelter your shelter

A good pitch will be shielded from the elements, especially the prevailing wind. The ground should be as flat as possible and fairly free from rocks, tussocks and humps. It should be well-drained and free from possible flooding. And a water supply should be handy; if not a stream, then a tap. Noise is best screened by trees as river rapids let alone the traffic on even a quiet country road can disturb your getting to sleep (let alone the sleep itself). Trees in fact give that vital protection from wind and rain, but avoid pitching directly beneath them. Branches can drop on the tent. So can raindrops, now swollen in size after dripping off foliage, and which go on dropping long after the rain has stopped. They also contain acidic gook that can damage tent materials.

Buildings, boulders, hedges—not to mention other natural bulwarks available in countryside—will also shield your tent from the wind. Remember, however, that hint in Chapter 5. You do, after all, only need protection that comes, say, waist high—just the height of your tent. Anything above that will make life more comfortable, but is not essential, and in a pinch you will find shelter from the apparently impossible when you look for such low-height ramparts that are always available.

### Test the camp bed springs

Your actual pitch is just the ground covered by your tent's groundsheet. That is the only amount of ground which needs to be flat when rolled upon by you. Virtually the size of a pocket handkerchief, and with care found anywhere. Even on a mountainside (something you can find out for yourself whenever among hills by ascending two or three hundred feet up any hillside above the road to where sheep tracks cross the slopes like the contour lines on a map; although the ground is tilted steeply the actual surface of these 'trods' is flat and quite big enough in places to pitch a small tent perfectly level).

When you have discovered a good pitch check that overnight rain will not flood you out. This may seem obvious on a riverbank where you can determine the height of previous flood levels by: 1) asking the farmer, and 2) locating scraps of driftwood on fences, bushes and trees. But even a camp site here could be flooded when the river level stays as it is, but your pitch is lying above a spring or in a hollow where rain water gathers. Limestone and chalk areas are notably treacherous in this respect. In fact there are streams which are not shown on the map in such regions because during dry summer months they disappear completely and you might never realise the perfect turf your tent is resting upon is indeed one of these waterways—until it rains.

'Test the spring in the ground' it said in Chapter 5. 'Spring' meaning, resilience to your body weight here. Now however you must think about springs literally. Is there any chance water could puddle up from beneath? The principle of how it works at its most drastic is the quicksand, but water could still fill your groundsheet from some underground source even though it isn't actually raining on your tent! (Build a quicksand for younger family members and see their amazement as an Action Man sinks out of sight in a biscuit tin full of sand, and you will understand even better. It's easy. Cut a one-inch diameter hole in the bottom of the tin and then punch another in one of the sides just below the rim. Place pieces of broken saucer, cup or plate over the bottom hole and fill the box with sand to a level just below the second hole you made. Now place the Action Man on top. Push the end of a hose through the top hole and soak the sand so it becomes compacted. Now switch the end of the hose to the bottom hole. This has the effect of an underground spring and the Action Man will sink.)

And the signs that your pitch might well become water-logged too? First of all look for obvious turn-offs like the edges of ponds full of water lilies, backwaters, sandbanks where willow and gorse flourish, long unkempt grass, thick under-growth in hollows, low-level meadows, and clayey soil. These places are chilly, damp and insects thrive here. But you must also be able to suss-out ground which floods fast, although it may be pepper-dry, warm to touch and insect-free now. Wild flowers and grasses can give you good clues here, and the illustration shows you what to look for. Yellow-green and bright green grasses are not so good, for example. Nor are reeds. Nor is moss on the ground. Clumpy grass flying white tips—cotton grass—is another plant which flourishes where the ground is like a sponge after rain. And the two carnivorous plants which eat insects—the butterwort and sundew (again as shown)—are also found in often-moist areas which might be dry now, but just wait for the rain! The butterwort snares flies which stick to the glue on its leaves, and these fold over to crush; sticky hairs, which curve inwards to trap the insects which it digests at leisure, are the secret of the sundew.

If the only ground available slopes, pick the gentlest part of the incline and pitch your tent at the top—wind direction permitting, so you can sleep head uphill. You might have to pitch the tent across wind (so long as the breeze cannot blow into the doorway). But some campers prefer setting their tent this way anyway rather than pitching the tail of the tent into the wind.

## CAMP SITE LIVING SYSTEMS

Your camping out experiences for the Hang Glider and Timberline tent experiments will have given you an inkling of the essentials here—like placing your cooking gear ready to the right (when you are not left-handed). Practice counts a lot, but the basic systems are listed below.

### Hitching tents together

A small tent on its own is in a similar position in bad weather to a spaceship—not much seperates the occupants from the enormous reality of what is just outside. It can have a bad psychological effect when rain and wind bottles you inside a capsule where you cannot stand but have to lie down, sit or crouch; your tent, in fact. Yet supposing you hitched (as well as pitched) two tents together? A School of Architecture has in fact designed a tent system on the lines of a space station where spaceships are plugged in on arrival. In this case five two-man tents are plugged into a large central 'mother' tent, the advantages being the small tents gave privacy; the larger one, centralised cooking, medicine and planning facilities. There is no feeling of being cut-off as happens to a pair of climbers, say, marooned for days in a blizzard on a high peak. And while this kind of consideration might not seem applicable to you, it does have some bearing on your safety.

Two tents pitched across the wind, their entrances hitched together, can work as an efficient door-to-door unit in bad weather. Although each tent is completely independent, the extra feeling of companionship gives an important boost. Meals can also be cooked quicker when each tent deals with one part of the meal seperately—the cookers, of course, being operated in the open and not inside the shelters.

In fine weather, however, tents are best kept as completely independent units, although the food can be prepared on both cookers at once for one big meal.

*Danger List of Camp Site Flowers*
*Top: Butterwort, Red Campion, Welsh Poppy, Common Sundew*
*Bottom: Globe Flower, Marsh Marigold, Angelica*

## Kit caching–1

For '1', read NOW. Unroll the sleeping bag and insulating pad as soon as possible and shake the bag to allow the filling to loft. Then lie the bag on the pad and your bed is ready.

Now sort out the rest.

Most gear will be stored beneath the flysheet or, in the case of a one-skinned tent, inside your pack or travel bags or whatever—until you need it. Anything which needs to go outside the tent, however, (and this still applies to gear stashed beneath the flysheet) should be wrapped in plastic bags and weighted down with heavy stones.

All you need inside the tent are: flashlight by the pillow; the pillow itself being clothes stuffed inside a tee-shirt or sweater; and pots, pans, water carrier and stove easily reached outside the tent. Food can be kept partly under the flysheet and partly in the tent depending on which items are most often used. Either way if you have to cook in the tent entrance it is easily reached.

Pull your canoe up to the bank. Then lift your gear out. The fact your canoe rests on dry land also means you can use it as invaluable storage space for items which would otherwise take up tent room. And on a windy night, or when it is impossible to push tent pegs into the ground (say you have to pitch an emergency camp on a concrete car park, and it has happened!) you will find your guys can be tied down to the canoes as well as large rocks—as you did for those experimental tents. The snags of having your canoe on the bank are that a wind in the night could bowl the glassfibre shell about—you should have tied it down first. Also, horses, cows etc. can cause damage to canoes. Check first for such livestock and put your canoes out of the way.

Hide your bike out of sight among trees or below a wall and chain it to something solid.

### Waterworks & sanitation department

Take water from your stream or river well upstream of your camp site. To check it is fit to drink you might get sound advice from locals, but to be really safe you should always boil water when you are unsure (for five minutes at least). Or make for the nearest tap water; most farms or houses will fill your container.

Choose a point further downstream of the tent, however, for washing water. You should also hack out a small pit in the ground nearby into which you can pour greasy, dirty water—replacing the sods back on top when you are leaving the camp site. Never throw debris from cooking pans and plates into the running water, but take the water out of the stream or river and wash over the 'grease pit'.

Your lavatory should be well away from the waterway and anyone else. All you need are lavatory paper, a hole and stones to cover the signs you have spent the night here.

### Tent tensioning

Adjust your tent so that nylon panels are strum-taut; and in the case of a cotton tent, there should be no more tension in the shelter than needed to prevent wrinkles—so there is room for the material to shrink when it becomes damp. Place rocks and spare pegs by strategic points around the tent in case you need reinforcements during a windy night. The pegs should be stuck in the ground by existing pegs, and the rocks are a last resort—as mentioned earlier they can chainsaw through guy lines quickly.

### Camp cooking

Cook outside (yourself as well as the cooker) when it is warm and the ground is dry; cook inside (but with your cooker outside the tent door, and you inside your sleeping bag), however, when it is raining. Pin the cooker to the ground with tent pegs, so that it cannot be knocked over easily.

### Kit caching–2

For '2', read LAST THING BEFORE RETIRING. Store the last of your gear last thing at night (or ready for the hot meal eaten in your sleeping bag when you arrive at a camp site in rain) to this sequence: Collect your water from stream or tap and bring it to the tent doorway; change from your wet clothes to dry clothes inside the doorway; pack the wet clothing in plastic bags outside; boots should also be stowed in a plastic bag; check all food is sealed in containers or plastic bags.

### Surviving the one-skin nylon tent

Main points, again, are: leave the door open all the time if possible (you can at least sleep with it partly open): keep your sponge by the flashlight in case you need to mop the tent insides during the night; sleep with your head underneath the gauze panel in the eaves so your warm breath is sucked out: plastic bags are 'musts' for storing damp clothing; old newspapers are good moppers-up when laid on the floor.

## CAMP SITE SECURITY

It is a shame when young people lose belongings on a camping trip. Yet the fact is that tent, sleeping bag and cooker are vulnerable—not to mention the canoes, bikes, cameras and other ancillary valuables which go with them. Yet often they are left lying unguarded and accessible to anyone loitering with intent (sorry about that) when, say, you are using your tent as a 'base camp' and have gone off walking, swimming or hang gliding for the day, leaving everything ready for your return that night.

A lot of outdoor gear goes missing from camp sites, especially in highly touristic districts where by no means every passer-by has your interests at heart. And you might well ask how best you can lock it up?

First, insure your tent, sleeping bag and other possessions likely to be used when camping. Secondly, take most of your valuables with you when you leave a base camp and plan to return in the evening. Your money, camera and sleeping bag, for instance. This last item may seem superfluous but there is a good reason. It will weigh little, yet help fill the empty spaces in your day sack *and* you always have it for an emergency. A sleeping bag in fact is required kit on expeditions from outdoor pursuits centres.

That leaves your tent standing alone, door fastened and nothing inside except food and cooker. The chances are everything will now still be there when you return in the evening.

## HOW TO GET THE BEST FROM ROTTEN WEATHER

Hills that look cut out of cereal packets, distant headlands which seem close enough to touch and cows galloping in fields . . . all are signs of approaching bad weather. You can beat the sinking feeling they bring with the right attitude. And you can even get some fun out of rain too. At the same time, however, you must recognise the danger in cold wet conditions. There is one risk in particular to be aware (and beware) of: hypothermia or, as it used to be called, exposure.

### The young person's guide to the temperature and wind chill chart

Cold, wet weather can chill the body and sap energy so thoroughly that before the victim knows it he is staggering around in a 'drunken' stupor—a sign of hypothermia, of which full details are given in *Survival for Young People*. It is often caused by insufficient food—no breakfast, say, and little eaten through the day. You gradually get weaker walking, cycling or canoeing and feel ready to collapse in wild countryside.

The golden rules are, of course, to eat a hot meal the night before, follow that next morning with breakfast and keep eating high-energy foods during the day. Drink water whenever you feel thirsty too. You also need the correct clothing—especially woollen garments which keep warm when wet. And your route should be short, low-level and certainly not strenuous in the first instances.

The simplest example of wind chill is felt whenever you test which way the wind is blowing. That's right, by holding up a wetted finger. If there is no breeze the finger feels quite normal, but even a light draught will chill part of the finger noticeably. Imagine that effect magnified many times more over your whole body when you are wet and you can see how weakening wetness plus wind can prove.

See for yourself, too, the real thing by carrying a cheap spirit thermometer—bought for under £1 from a garden centre or Woolworths—in the experiment below when you choose a wet day to go walking. Stop occasionally to take the air temperature by shielding the thermometer from any breeze with your body. Then look for signs of wind speed as given in the chart by the Beaufort Wind Scale (used by Naval officers who, like fishermen, are supposed to exaggerate everything: hence this chart whose purpose is to hold that imagination in check) and you will see how quickly the danger zone is reached with a coldish temperature and brisk wind.

The risk is heightened by wind. As the temperature and wind chill chart shows you are then much more at risk for while the temperature on its own may be nothing serious, a wind blowing as well will lower it appreciably. Always be ready for this danger when camping and if necessary cut your intended route short when conditions worsen. It is better that your route suffers rather than you do. Certainly you must stop and camp early if any of your group are showing signs of becoming tired.

# THE YOUNG PERSON'S TEMPERATURE & WIND CHILL CHART

**COOLING POWER OF WIND EXPRESSED AS "EQUIVALENT CHILL TEMPERATURE"**

EQUIVALENT CHILL TEMPERATURE

| WIND SPEED (APPROX) | TEMPERATURE (°F) | | | | | | | | | | | | | | | | | | | | |
|---|---|---|---|---|---|---|---|---|---|---|---|---|---|---|---|---|---|---|---|---|---|
| | 40 | 35 | 30 | 25 | 20 | 15 | 10 | 5 | 0 | -5 | -10 | -15 | -20 | -25 | -30 | -35 | -40 | -45 | -50 | -55 | -60 |
| **Calm:** no chill felt on wet finger when raised high | 40 | 35 | 30 | 25 | 20 | 15 | 10 | 5 | 0 | -5 | -10 | -15 | -20 | -25 | -30 | -35 | -40 | -45 | -50 | -55 | -60 |
| **Light Breeze** (5mph): waterproofs rustle when you stop; wind felt on face; leaves stir | 35 | 30 | 25 | 20 | 15 | 10 | 5 | 0 | -5 | -10 | -15 | -20 | -25 | -30 | -35 | -40 | -45 | -50 | -55 | -65 | -70 |
| **Gentle Breeze** (10mph): maps flutter when read; hair blows; leaves and twigs move; and bracken too | 30 | 20 | 15 | 10 | 5 | 0 | -10 | -15 | -20 | -25 | -35 | -40 | -45 | -50 | -60 | -65 | -70 | -75 | -80 | -90 | -95 |
| **Moderate Breeze** (15mph): anorak hood 'windsocks'; small branches lifted; rucksack straps blow out; loose paper blown away | 25 | 15 | 10 | 0 | -5 | -10 | -20 | -25 | -30 | -40 | -45 | -50 | -60 | -65 | -70 | -80 | -85 | -90 | -100 | -105 | -110 |
| **Fresh Breeze** (20mph): small trees in leaf begin to sway; catspaws ripple across water; hard to cycle against | 20 | 10 | 5 | 0 | -10 | -15 | -25 | -30 | -35 | -45 | -50 | -60 | -65 | -75 | -80 | -85 | -95 | -100 | -110 | -115 | -120 |
| **Strong Breeze** (25mph): large branches in motion; hats blow off; tents difficult to pitch when in exposed positions; telegraph wires whistle | 15 | 10 | 0 | -5 | -15 | -20 | -30 | -35 | -45 | -50 | -60 | -65 | -75 | -80 | -90 | -95 | -105 | -110 | -120 | -125 | -135 |
| **Moderate Gale** (35mph): whole trees sway; difficult to walk against; need to follow that advice about facing the right way to put on an anorak in a wind on pages 90 and 91 | 10 | 5 | 0 | -10 | -15 | -25 | -30 | -40 | -50 | -55 | -65 | -70 | -80 | -85 | -95 | -100 | -110 | -115 | -125 | -130 | -140 |
| **Fresh Gale** (40mph): twigs break off trees; high skylines unsafe; ferns, grasses, bracken, wool whirled high | 10 | 5 | -5 | -10 | -20 | -30 | -35 | -40 | -50 | -60 | -65 | -75 | -80 | -90 | -100 | -105 | -115 | -120 | -130 | -135 | -145 |
| **Strong Gale** (50mph): chimney pots and slates blown down; walkers need to link arms on high exposed ground and get lower; tents unprotected by lee of wall/boulder/tree etc likely to blow down too | 10 | 0 | -5 | -15 | -20 | -30 | -35 | -45 | -55 | -60 | -70 | -75 | -85 | -90 | -100 | -110 | -115 | -125 | -130 | -140 | -150 |

Winds above 40 have little additional effect

| LITTLE DANGER | INCREASING DANGER (Flesh may freeze within 1 min) | GREAT DANGER (Flesh may freeze within 30 seconds) |
|---|---|---|

## The walking-in-the-rain-for-the-sake-of-getting-wet-camping excursion

This is not as mad as it sounds. A walk in the rain, a warm night's sleep in your sleeping bag and then away again next morning in soaking-wet-through clothes is a good experience, and teaches you that rain can be coped with.

Choose two days when the weather forecast heralds rain, and plan an overnight camp near a road. Then collect your backpacking equipment. You will need raingear from the start, but do not wear too much. For instance, long johns, long wool socks and over-trousers might be one choice for the lower part of the body. Or, instead, climbing breeches, long wool socks and over trousers. And for the top? String vest, wool shirt, sweater and anorak or cagoule.

The danger of walking in the rain, wind and cold seems remote as you begin to enjoy it! The movement of your body creates a glow which is all the more invigorating once you have got wet and are literally soaking. The food you are chewing as well continually stokes this inner surface, and you are conscious of a real challenge in riding—walking, actually—this bad weather.

It is when you stop, of course, that your body heat begins to run down and you are conscious of wet clammy clothing—especially if it is windy and the air currents penetrate and carry away your vital body warmth. Know your drill, however, and organise your camp quickly on arrival at your pitch.

Take the tent from the top of the rucksack and pitch it. Then carry out the sequence mentioned above of emptying your rucksack, going for water, then stripping off the wet clothing and climbing into your warm dry spare clothing carried in the sack. You can now arrange your gear for the night, climb inside the sleeping bag—sodden garments squeezed and wrung out, then packed into a plastic bag which is put outside the tent—and begin cooking.

Next morning is the crunch. Hope it is still raining to make things as life-like as possible. Fine weather, however, can still be countered with the wet clothing you wore the day before and which you must now put on again. Why not wear the dry clothing you might ask? If it is raining, however, those dry garments will soon be as wet as your already-soaked clothes, and then you will have no dry clothing in reserve at all. And even though it may be a fine morning now, who is to say it will not rain in an hour or so? So it has to be the wet clothes again, and the really tough part is climbing into them. However, a system again helps.

First, brew up coffee or tea from the warmth of your sleeping bag. Then cook breakfast. Clean out the tent after this and pack everything you can inside the rucksack without going outside. This leaves the tent and dry clothes still to pack. Quickly strip off your dry clothing, and stash it away. You must slip the wet clothing back on—and quickly. It is like a cold shower: there is a sudden shock to your system, but in seconds you have accepted it. Your skin is water resistant and so long as you keep moving you will not catch cold. Go to work taking down the tent now, packing everything finally away and clearing up the site and your body will be glowing again so effectively that if it is not actually raining body warmth alone will dry out the most sodden clothes in two hours. Of course, you will have to give it every chance from the open air too. Pack the waterproofs away until it rains again.

## EMERGENCIES CAUSED BY BAD WEATHER

Sunstroke (when your blood boils) and snakes (they can slip into empty anorak sleeves thrown down on the grass as you rest) are hazards you have a good chance of avoiding. Bad weather, however, creates more crises, and all the time. And you should be ready for them from the beginning.

### Money soaking wet

Wet pound notes and dollar bills should not be separated until they have dried out, then they peel apart easily. Keep the bits if you accidentally tear them as you can claim new banknotes at the bank with the remnants of the damaged ones.

### Tent leaks

There are various solutions. Draw a finger down the inside of the fabric from where the drips drop, and the water will be diverted down this channel. Or use warm wax from a hot candle (CARE!). Elastoplast or canoe tape stuck over the hole will also make a temporary repair.

### Sleet drums the pot on the cooker

Let it. So long as a lid covers the contents, and your stove has a windshield and / or large stones sheltering it from the wind, you can still cook outside the tent doorway.

### A gale flies your tent like a windsock while you pitch it

One person should concentrate on pitching one end while the other lies on the tent and pins it to the ground. Then the other end can be pitched under tension from the first-pitched end.

### Something catches fire inside your tent

Smother it immediately with your sleeping bag or any handy piece of cloth or clothing. This will not damage the fabric, but will save the situation—when done firmly and promptly. To avoid this break all long candles in half as they often get knocked over and start internal fires. Go outside if the insulating pad ever comes into contact with flames; it can produce dangerous fumes from the plastic foam.

### The tent catches fire

Get outside fast. Collapse the poles and, if necessary, the main guys to smother the flames. Any other way is too slow. Exterior poles make flattening the tent to the ground even quicker.

### Your stove goes up in flames in the tent doorway

Boot it out or throw it well clear when you can no longer control the burning.

### You catch fire

Roll over and over on the ground at once. Wrap anything around you which would help smother the flames. Never stand up as the flames can run up past your face like a torch.

### Someone else catches fire

Knock them down and smother the flames with the sleeping bag or even by lying on top of the burning part yourself.

### You wake up with the candle out and a headache from the fug inside the tent

This happens when you have not ventilated your tent properly with two seperate openings which allows fresh air to circulate. It is accelerated in stormy weather when the door is zipped tight, and you may have brought the cooker inside the tent to finish cooking your meal—against previous advice. Carbon monoxide is created in the closed atmosphere, and can asphyxiate tent occupants. Get out fast into fresh air when you suspect lack of ventilation is the cause. Another sign is that stoves burn inside a tent with a yellow flame rather than a blue one.

Also beware of gas leaking from containers if you have a cooker burning too near or even inside the tent: they should be stored OUTside. The modern tray or bathtub groundsheet will trap gas which is heavier than air that much more easily, and the gas level could rise to your nose as you sleep—as well as explode if you strike a match.

### You are flooded out

Pack your sleeping bag away first thing in case you have a chance of saving it from the water. The last resort when everything is waterlogged and it is still the middle of the night is to put on what dry clothes you have left. And sit it out in your plastic bivi bag—actually sitting on a seat improvised from anything which will keep you from touching the ground; plastic food boxes, say, or your rucksack. Wear your anorak but hold your arms beneath the armpits rather than slipping them inside the sleeves as this keeps you all the warmer.

## PACKING UP TO GO

You have done this before at the beginning of the book. A last stressing, however: leave your site looking as if you have never been there. Take all your litter home in a plastic bag included empty tins which you have smashed flat with rocks. And pay the farmer on your way.

## WHEN YOU GET BACK HOME . . .

There are three main things to do apart from sorting out and cleaning of your equipment.

### See to your tent

If a wet tent is left rolled up it will begin to rot, crack, shrink, creep and generally deteriorate. A wet tent should be opened up within twelve hours, whether on another site or back home. And a good way to do this if you have a lawn is to pitch it there and leave it until fine weather blows it dry. Otherwise sponge off any mud and soil now, and give it a good shake. Then drape it over a table or hang it up, the guys tied to different objects so the material is spread out and has the best chance of drying quickly. You can do this in a garage, an attic or over the kitchen table. If indoors, however, spread newspaper on the floor to catch the drips. A cotton tent, incidentally, should have its mud left intact as this is more easily brushed off when dry. Check carefully there is no mud or dirt in the zip. If this item becomes clogged it is most likely to jam. Clean with a damp cloth, and brush when dry with stiff bristled brush.

As the material dries out use a vacuum cleaner nozzle to remove grit and dirt from seams, folds and the groundsheet. When dry do a final brushing over, and sponge down to remove any stains and fold away—checking too that seams, folds and even the guys are dry. See that guys, for instance, are not too worn, that the stitching is intact along the seams and that any half-broken rubber guys are replaced. Straighten the tent pegs and clean with a lightly oiled rag.

### Unroll the sleeping bag

Fold it loosely and store it in a warm, dry cupboard.

### Find the rejects

Sort the gear you took into two lots. One is the equipment you used; the other, the gear you didn't. Think hard before taking any of that second lot with you again.

# INDEX